COACHING YOUTH

TENNIS

SECOND EDITION

American Sport Education Program

in cooperation with the
United States Tennis Association

Human Kinetics

Library of Congress Cataloging-in-Publication Data

American Sport Education Program.
    Coaching youth tennis / American Sport Education Program in cooperation with
the United States Tennis Association. -- 2nd ed.
      p. cm.
    Rev. ed. of: Rookie coaches tennis guide. ©1991.
    ISBN 0-87322-966-5 (pbk.)
    1. Tennis--Coaching.   2. Tennis for children--Coaching.
I. United States Tennis Association. II. American Sport Education
Program. Rookie coaches tennis guide. III. Title.
GV1002.9.C63A45   1998
796.342'07'7--dc21   97-52260
                                                  CIP

ISBN: 0-87322-966-5

This book is the second edition of *Rookie Coaches Tennis Guide*.

Acquisitions Editor: Jim Kestner; **Tennis Consultant:** Karen Ford; **Managing Editor:**
Coree Schutter; **Assistant Editor:** Jennifer Brooke Jackson; **Copyeditor:** Bonnie Pettifor;
Proofreader: Erin Cler; **Graphic Designers:** Judy Henderson and Nancy Rasmus; **Graphic
Artist:** Francine Hamerski; **Cover Designer:** Stuart Cartwright; **Photographer (cover):**
United States Tennis Association; **Illustrators:** Keith Blomberg and Paul To, line draw-
ings; Studio 2D and Nancy Rasmus, Mac art; **Printer:** United Graphics

Copies of this book are available at special discounts for bulk purchase for sales promotions,
premiums, fund-raising, or educational use. Special editions or book excerpts can also be
created to specifications. For details, contact the Special Sales Manager at Human Kinetics.

Printed in the United States of America   10 9 8 7 6 5 4 3 2

Human Kinetics
Web site: http://www.humankinetics.com/

United States: Human Kinetics, P.O. Box 5076, Champaign, IL 61825-5076
1-800-747-4457

Canada: Human Kinetics, 475 Devonshire Road, Unit 100, Windsor, ON N8Y 2L5
1-800-465-7301 (in Canada only)

Europe: Human Kinetics, P.O. Box IW14, Leeds LS16 6TR, United Kingdom
+44 (0)113-278 1708

Australia: Human Kinetics, 57A Price Avenue, Lower Mitcham, South Australia 5062
(08) 82771555

New Zealand: Human Kinetics, P.O. Box 105-231, Auckland Central
09-523-3462

Contents

A Word From the USTA

As Director of Coaching for the United States Tennis Association Player Development Program, I applaud your interest in helping young Americans learn the fun and challenging game of tennis. As a tennis coach, you will have the opportunity to introduce a sport to children that they can enjoy for the rest of their lives.

Coaching Youth Tennis, Second Edition will be an invaluable resource for you. The practical, step-by-step information provided will make you feel well qualified even if you've never coached before. In fact, this book was designed specifically for novice coaches! All of your concerns have been addressed. You'll understand the importance of your role as a coach; how to communicate effectively with your players; the best way to teach new skills and organize on-court drills; how to promote team spirit; and basic first aid and sport science concepts.

The knowledge you are gaining has an instant application for a new USTA tennis program as well. Coaches such as you are currently introducing thousands of youngsters across the country to **USA Junior Team Tennis.** This program provides a team opportunity for fun, fitness, and friendship while promoting the philosophy of Fundamentals, Fair & Equal Play, Appropriate Groupings, and Positive Coaching. I encourage all of you to become involved.

On behalf of the United States Tennis Association, I welcome you to coaching and wish you fun and personal fulfillment in your new role.

Stan Smith
USTA Director
of Coaching

Welcome to Coaching!

Coaching young people is an exciting way to be involved in sport. But it isn't easy. The untrained novice coach or parent may be overwhelmed by the responsibilities involved in helping players through their early tennis experiences. Preparing youngsters physically and mentally in tennis and providing them with a positive role model are among the difficult—but rewarding—tasks you will assume.

This book will help you meet the challenges and experience the rewards of coaching young athletes. We call it *Coaching Youth Tennis* because it is intended for coaches and parents who are working with developing tennis players. In this book you'll learn how to apply general coaching principles and teach tennis rules, skills, and strategies successfully to kids. This book also serves as a text for the American Sport Education Program's (ASEP) Coaching Youth Sport Course.

We hope you will find coaching rewarding and that you will continue to learn more about coaching and tennis so that you can be the best possible coach for your young athletes.

If you would like more information about ASEP and its Coaching Youth Sport Course, please contact us at

ASEP
P.O. Box 5076
Champaign, IL 61825-5076
1-800-747-5698
asep@hkusa.com
http://www.asep.com/

Good Coaching!

Who, Me . . . a Coach?

If you are like most youth coaches, you have probably been recruited from the ranks of concerned parents, sport enthusiasts, or community volunteers. And, like many coaches, you probably have had little formal instruction on how to coach. But when the call went out for coaches to assist with the local youth tennis program, you answered because you like children and enjoy tennis, and perhaps are interested in starting a coaching career.

I Want to Help, but . . .

Your initial coaching assignment may be difficult. Like many volunteers, you may not know everything there is to know about tennis, nor about how to work with children between the ages of 7 and 14. Relax, because *Coaching Youth Tennis* will help you learn the basics for coaching tennis effectively. In the coming pages you will find the answers to such common questions as these:

- What tools do I need to be a good coach?
- How can I best communicate with my players?
- How do I go about teaching sport skills?
- What can I do to promote safety?
- What should I do when someone is injured?
- What are the basic rules, skills, and strategies of tennis?
- What practice drills will improve my players' skills?

Before answering these questions, let's take a look at what's involved in being a coach.

Am I a Parent or a Coach?

Many coaches are parents, but the two roles should not be confused. Unlike your role as a parent, as a coach you are responsible not only to yourself and your child, but also to the organization, all the players on the team (including your child), and their parents. Because of this additional responsibility, your behavior during your players' matches will be different from your behavior at home, and your son or daughter may not understand why.

For example, imagine the confusion of a young boy who is the center of his parents' attention at home but is barely noticed by his father/coach in the sport setting. Or consider the mixed signals received by a young girl whose tennis skill is constantly evaluated by a mother/coach who otherwise rarely comments on her daughter's activities. You need to explain to your son or daughter your new responsibilities and how they will affect your relationship when coaching.

Take the following steps to avoid such problems in coaching your child:

- Ask your child if he or she wants you to coach the team.
- Explain why you wish to be involved with the team.
- Discuss with your child how your interactions will change when you take on the role of coach at practices or games.
- Limit your coaching behavior to when you are in the coaching role.
- Avoid parenting during practice or game situations, to keep your role clear in your child's mind.
- Reaffirm your love for your child, regardless of his or her performance on the tennis court.

What Are My Responsibilities as a Coach?

A coach assumes the responsibility of doing everything possible to ensure that the youngsters on his or her team will have an enjoyable and safe sporting experience while they learn sport skills. If you're ever in doubt about your approach, remind yourself that "fun and fundamentals" are most important.

Provide an Enjoyable Experience

Tennis should be fun. Even if nothing else is accomplished, make certain your players have fun. Take the fun out of sport and you'll take the kids out of sport.

Children enter sport for a number of reasons (e.g., to meet and play with other children, to develop physically, and to learn skills), but their major objective is to have fun. Help them satisfy this goal by injecting humor and variety into your practices. Also, make matches nonthreatening, festive experiences for your players. Such an approach will increase your players' desire to participate in the future, which should be the biggest goal of youth sport. Unit 2 will help you learn how to satisfy your players' yearning for fun and keep winning in perspective. And unit 3 will describe how you can effectively communicate this perspective to them.

Provide a Safe Experience

You are responsible for planning and teaching activities in such a way that the progression between activities minimizes risks (see units 4 and 5). Further, you must ensure that the courts on which your team practices and plays, and the equipment team members use, are free of hazards. Finally, you need to protect yourself from any legal liability issues that might arise from your involvement as a coach. Unit 5 will help you take the appropriate precautions.

Provide Opportunities for Children With Disabilities

There's a possibility that a child with a disability of some kind will register for your team. Don't panic! Your youth sport administrator or a number of organizations can provide you with information to help you best meet this child's needs.

As a coach, you need to know about the Americans with Disabilities Act (ADA). Passed in 1990, the ADA gives individuals the same legal protection against discrimination on the basis of disabilities as is provided against discrimination on the basis of race, gender, and class. The law does recognize that there are times when including an individual who is disabled might risk the safety of that individual and other players, but the exact way that courts are treating the ADA is still being decided. In general, the law requires that "reasonable accommodations" be made to include children with disabilities into organized sport programs. If a parent or child approaches you on the subject, and you aren't sure what to do, talk to the director in charge of your tennis program. If you make any decision on your own pertaining to the ADA, you may be vulnerable to a lawsuit.

Keep in mind that these children want to participate alongside their able-bodied peers. Give them the same support and encouragement that you give other athletes, and model their inclusion and acceptance for all your athletes.

Teach Basic Tennis Skills

In becoming a coach, you take on the role of educator. You must teach your players the fundamental skills and strategies necessary for success in tennis. That means that you need to "go to school."

If you don't know the basics of tennis now, you can learn them by reading the second half of this book, units 6, 7, and 8. But even if you know tennis as a player, do you know how to teach it? This book will help you get started. There are also many valuable tennis books on the market, including those offered by Human Kinetics. See the list of books in the back of this book or call (800) 747-4457 for more information.

You'll also find it easier to provide good educational experiences for your players if you plan your practices. Unit 4 of this book provides some guidelines for planning effective practices.

Getting Help

Veteran coaches in your league are an especially good source of help for you. These coaches have all experienced the same emotions and concerns you are facing, and their advice and feedback can be invaluable as you work through your first season.

You can also learn a lot by watching local high school and college tennis coaches in practices and games. You might even ask a few of the coaches you respect most to lend you a hand with a couple of your practices. You can get additional help by attending tennis clinics, reading tennis publications, and studying instructional videos. In addition to the American Sport Education Program (ASEP), the following national organization will assist you in obtaining more tennis coaching information:

> United States Tennis Association
> 70 W. Red Oak Lane
> White Plains, NY 10604
> Phone: (914) 696-7000
> Fax: (914) 696-7167

Coaching tennis is a rewarding experience. And, just as you want your players to practice and learn to be the best they can be, you need to learn all you can about coaching in order to be the best tennis coach you can be.

What Tools Do I Need as a Coach?

Have you purchased the traditional coaching tools—things like tennis balls, a whistle, a clipboard, and a first aid kit? They'll help you coach, but to be a successful coach you'll need five other tools that cannot be bought. These tools are available only through self-examination and hard work; they're easy to remember using the acronym COACH:

> **C**—Comprehension
>
> **O**—Outlook
>
> **A**—Affection
>
> **C**—Character
>
> **H**—Humor

Comprehension

Comprehension of the rules, skills, and tactics of tennis is required. To help you learn about the game, the second half of this book describes how it is played as well as specific techniques and strategies. In the tennis-specific section of this book, you'll also find a variety of drills to use in developing young players' skills. And, perhaps most important, you'll learn how to apply your knowledge of the game to teach your tennis team.

To improve your comprehension of tennis, take the following steps:

- Read the tennis-specific section of this book.
- Read other tennis coaching books, including those available from ASEP (see the back of this book for more information).
- Contact the United States Tennis Association (see page 7).
- Attend tennis coaches' clinics.
- Talk with other, more experienced coaches.
- Observe local college, high school, and youth tennis matches.
- Watch televised tennis matches.

In addition to having tennis knowledge, you must implement proper training and safety methods so your players can participate with little risk of injury. Even then, sport injuries will occur. And more often than not, you'll be the first person responding to your players' injuries, so be sure you understand the basic emergency care procedures described in unit 5. Also, read in that unit how to handle more serious sport injury situations.

Outlook

Outlook refers to your perspective and goals—what you are seeking as a coach. The most common coaching objectives are (a) to have fun, (b) to help players develop their physical, mental, and social skills, and (c) to win. Thus your outlook involves the priorities you set, your planning, and your vision for the future.

To work successfully with children in a sport setting, you must have your priorities in order. In just what order do you rank the importance of fun, development, and winning?

Answer the following questions to examine your objectives:

Of which situation would you be most proud?
   a. Knowing that each participant enjoyed playing tennis.
   b. Seeing that all players improved their tennis skills.
   c. Winning the league championship.

Which statement best reflects your thoughts about sport?
   a. If it isn't fun, don't do it.
   b. Everyone should learn something every day.
   c. Sport isn't fun if you don't win.

How would you like your players to remember you?
   a. As a coach who was fun to play for.
   b. As a coach who provided a good base of fundamental skills.
   c. As a coach who had a winning record.

Which would you most like to hear a parent of a child on your team say?
   a. Billy really had a good time playing tennis this year.
   b. Susie learned some important lessons playing tennis this year.
   c. Jose played on the first-place tennis team this year.

Which of the following would be the most rewarding moment of your season?
   a. Having your team want to continue playing, even after practice is over.

    b. Seeing your players learn how to get off accurately placed first serves.

    c. Winning a match on a strategy you directed.

Look over your answers. If you most often selected "a" responses, then having fun is most important to you. A majority of "b" answers suggests that skill development is what attracts you to coaching. And if "c" was your most frequent response, winning is tops on your list of coaching priorities.

Most coaches say fun and development are more important, but when actually coaching, some coaches emphasize—indeed, overemphasize—winning. You, too, will face situations that challenge you to keep winning in its proper perspective. During such moments, you'll have to choose between emphasizing your players' development or winning. If your priorities are in order, your players' well-being will take precedence over your team's win-loss record every time.

Take the following actions to better define your outlook:

1. Determine your priorities for the season.
2. Prepare for situations that challenge your priorities.
3. Set goals for yourself and your players that are consistent with those priorities.
4. Plan how you and your players can best attain those goals.
5. Review your goals frequently to be sure that you are staying on track.

It is particularly important for coaches to permit all young athletes to participate. Each youngster—male or female, small or tall, gifted or disabled—should have an opportunity to develop skills and have fun.

Remember that the challenge and joy of sport is experienced through striving to win, not through winning itself. Players who aren't allowed on the court are denied the opportunity to strive to win. And herein lies the irony: Coaches who allow all of their players to participate and develop skills will—in the end—come out on top.

ASEP has a motto that will help you keep your outlook in the best interest of the kids on your team. It summarizes in four words all you need to remember when establishing your coaching priorities:

Athletes First,

Winning Second

This motto recognizes that striving to win is an important, even vital, part of sport. But it emphatically states that no efforts in striving to win should be made at the expense of the athletes' well-being, development, and enjoyment.

Affection

Affection is another vital tool you will want to have in your coaching kit: a genuine concern for the young people you coach. It involves having a love for children, a desire to share with them your love and knowledge of tennis, and the patience and understanding that allow each individual playing for you to grow from his or her involvement in tennis.

Successful coaches have a real concern for the health and welfare of their players. They care that each child on the team has an enjoyable and successful experience. They recognize that there are similarities between young people's sport experiences and other activities in their lives, and they encourage their players to strive to learn from all their experiences, to become well-rounded individuals. These coaches have a strong desire to work with children and be involved in their growth. They also have the patience to work with those who are slower to learn or less capable of performing. If you have such qualities or are willing to work hard to develop them, then you have the affection necessary to coach young athletes.

There are many ways to demonstrate your affection and patience, including these:

- Make an effort to get to know each player on your team.
- Treat each player as an individual.
- Empathize with players trying to learn new and difficult skills.
- Treat players as you would like to be treated under similar circumstances.
- Be in control of your emotions.
- Show your enthusiasm for being involved with your team.

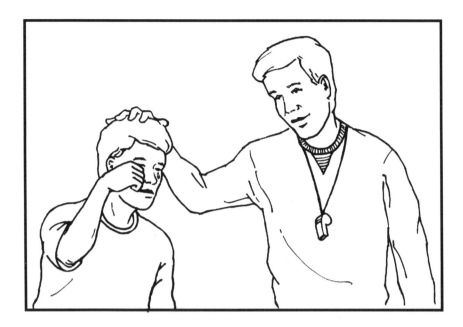

- Keep an upbeat and positive tone in all of your communications.

Some children appreciate a pat on the back or shoulder as a sign of your approval or affection. But be aware that not all players feel comfortable with being touched. When this is the case, you need to respect their wishes.

Character

Character is a word that adults use frequently in conversations about sport experiences and young people. If you haven't already, you may one day be asked to explain whether you think sport builds good character. What will you say?

The fact that you have decided to coach young tennis players probably means that you think participation in sport is important. But whether or not that participation develops character in your players depends as much on you as it does on the sport itself. How can you build character in your players?

Youngsters learn by listening to what adults say. But they learn even more by watching the behavior of certain important individuals. As a coach, you are likely to be a significant figure in the lives of your players. Will you be a good role model?

Having good character means modeling appropriate behaviors for sports and life. That means more than just saying the right things. What you say and what you do must match. There is no place in coaching for the "Do as I say, not as I do" philosophy. Challenge, support, encourage, and reward every child, and your players will be more likely to accept, even celebrate, their differences. Be in control before, during, and after all matches and practices. And don't be afraid to admit that you were wrong. No one is perfect!

Many of us have been coached by someone who believes that criticizing players is a good way to build character. In reality, this approach damages children's self-esteem and teaches them that their value as a person is based on how they perform in sports. Unit 3 will help you communicate with your players in a way that builds positive self-esteem and develops your athletes' skills.

Finally, take stock of your own attitudes about ethnic, gender, and other stereotypes. You are an individual coach, and it would be wrong for others to form beliefs about you based on their personal attitudes about coaches in general. Similarly, you need to avoid making comments that support stereotypes of others. Let your words and actions show your players that every individual matters, and you will be teaching them a valuable lesson about respecting and supporting individuals' differences.

Consider the following steps to being a good role model:

- Take stock of your strengths and weaknesses.
- Build on your strengths.
- Set goals for yourself to improve upon those areas you would not like to see mimicked.
- If you slip up, apologize to your team and to yourself. You'll do better next time.

Humor

Humor is an often overlooked coaching tool. For our use it means having the ability to laugh at yourself and with your players during practices and matches. Nothing helps balance the tone of a serious, skill-learning session like a chuckle or two. And a sense of humor puts in perspective the many mistakes your young players will make. So don't get upset over each miscue or respond negatively to erring players. Allow your players and yourself to enjoy the ups, and don't dwell on the downs.

Here are some tips for injecting humor into your practices:

- Make practices fun by including a variety of activities.
- Keep all players involved in drills and scrimmages.
- Consider laughter by your players as a sign of enjoyment, not waning discipline.
- Smile!

Where Do You Stand?

To take stock of your "coaching tool kit," rank yourself on the three questions for each of the five coaching tools. Simply circle the number that best describes your current status on each item.

Not at all		Somewhat		Very much so
1	**2**	**3**	**4**	**5**

Comprehension

1. Could you explain the rules of tennis to other parents without studying for a long time?   1 2 3 4 5

2. Do you know how to organize and conduct safe practices?   1 2 3 4 5

3. Do you know how to provide first aid for most common, minor sport injuries?   1 2 3 4 5

Comprehension Score: _____

Outlook

4. Do you place the interests of all children ahead of winning when you coach?   1 2 3 4 5

5. Do you plan for every meeting, practice, and game?   1 2 3 4 5

6. Do you have a vision of what you want your players to be able to do by the end of the season?   1 2 3 4 5

Outlook Score: _____

Affection

7. Do you enjoy working with children?   1 2 3 4 5

8. Are you patient with youngsters who are learning new skills?   1 2 3 4 5

9. Are you able to show your players that you care?   1 2 3 4 5

Affection Score: _____

Character

10. Are your words and behaviors consistent with each other?   1 2 3 4 5
11. Are you a good model for your players?   1 2 3 4 5
12. Do you keep negative emotions under control before, during, and after games?   1 2 3 4 5

Character Score: _____

Humor

13. Do you usually smile at your players?   1 2 3 4 5
14. Are your practices fun?   1 2 3 4 5
15. Are you able to laugh at your mistakes?   1 2 3 4 5

Humor Score: _____

If you scored 9 or less on any of the coaching tools, be sure to reread those sections carefully. And even if you scored 15 on each tool, don't be complacent. Keep learning! Then you'll be well-equipped with the tools you need to coach young athletes.

Unit 3

How Should I Communicate With My Players?

Now you know the tools needed to COACH: Comprehension, Outlook, Affection, Character, and Humor. These are essentials for effective coaching; without them, you'd have a difficult time getting started. But none of those tools will work if you don't know how to use them with your athletes—and this requires skillful communication. This unit examines what communication is and how you can become a more effective communicator-coach.

What's Involved in Communication?

Coaches often mistakenly believe that communication involves only instructing players to do something, but verbal commands are a very small part of the communication process. More than half of what is communicated is nonverbal. So remember when you are coaching: Actions speak louder than words.

Communication in its simplest form is like one doubles player to the other. It involves two people: one to pass the message (verbally, through facial expression, and via body language) and the other to receive it. Of course, a player who fails to pay attention or judge the message correctly will not catch it.

How Can I Send More Effective Messages?

Young athletes often have little understanding of the rules and skills of tennis and probably even less confidence in playing it. So they need accurate, understandable, and supportive messages to help them along. That's why your verbal and nonverbal messages are so important.

Verbal Messages

"Sticks and stones may break my bones, but words will never hurt me" isn't true. Spoken words can have a strong and long-lasting effect. Coaches' words are particularly influential because youngsters place great importance on what coaches say. Perhaps you, like many former youth sport participants, have a difficult time remembering much of anything you were told by your elementary school teachers but can still recall several specific things your coaches at that level said to you. Such is the lasting effect of a coach's comments to a player.

Whether you are correcting misbehavior, teaching a player how to serve, or praising a player for good effort, there are a number of things you should consider when sending a message verbally. They include the following:

- *Be positive and honest.*
- *State it clearly and simply.*
- *Say it loud enough, and say it again.*
- *Be consistent.*

Be Positive and Honest

Nothing turns people off like hearing someone nag all the time, and young athletes react similarly to a coach who gripes constantly. Kids particularly need encouragement because many of them doubt their ability to play tennis. So look for and tell your players what they did well.

But don't cover up poor or incorrect play with rosy words of praise. Kids know all too well when they've erred, and no cheerfully expressed cliché can undo their mistakes. If you fail to acknowledge players' errors, your athletes will think you are a phony.

State It Clearly and Simply

Positive and honest messages are good, but only if expressed directly in words your players understand. "Beating around the bush" is ineffective and inefficient. And if you do ramble, your players will miss the point of your message and probably lose interest. Here are some tips for saying things clearly:

- Organize your thoughts before speaking to your athletes.
- Explain things thoroughly, but don't bore them with long-winded monologues.

- Use language your players can understand. However, avoid trying to be hip by using their age group's slang vocabulary.

COMPLIMENT SANDWICH

A good way to handle situations in which you have identified and must correct improper technique is to serve your players a "compliment sandwich":

1. Point out what the athlete did correctly.
2. Let the player know what was incorrect in the performance and instruct him or her how to correct it.
3. Encourage the player by reemphasizing what he or she did well.

Say It Loud Enough, and Say It Again

Talk to your team in a voice that all members can hear and interpret. A crisp, vigorous voice commands attention and respect; garbled and weak speech is tuned out. It's OK, in fact, appropriate, to soften your voice when speaking to a player individually about a personal problem. But most of the time your messages will be for all your players to hear, so make sure they can! An enthusiastic voice also motivates players and tells them you enjoy being their coach. A word of caution, however: Don't dominate the setting with a booming voice that distracts attention from players' performances.

Sometimes what you say, even if stated loudly and clearly, won't sink in the first time. This may be particularly true with young athletes hearing words they don't understand. To avoid boring repetition and yet still get your message across, say the same thing in a slightly different way. For instance, you might first tell your players "Follow through on your groundstrokes." Soon afterward, remind them "Swing right through the ball when hitting a groundstroke from the baseline." The second form of the message may get through to players who missed it the first time around.

Be Consistent

People often say things in ways that imply a different message. For example, a touch of sarcasm added to the words "way to go" sends an entirely different message than the words themselves suggest. It is essential that you avoid sending such mixed messages. Keep the tone of your voice consistent with the words you use. And don't say something one day and contradict it the next; players will get confused. If you still aren't certain whether your players understand, ask them to repeat the message back to you. As the old saying goes "If they can't say it, they can't play it."

Nonverbal Messages

Just as you should be consistent in the tone of voice and words you use, you should also keep your verbal and nonverbal messages consistent. An extreme example of failing to do this would be shaking your head, indicating disapproval, while at the same time telling a player "Nice try." Which is the player to believe, your gesture or your words?

Messages can be sent nonverbally in a number of ways. Facial expressions and body language are just two of the more obvious forms of nonverbal signals that can help you when you coach.

Facial Expressions

The look on a person's face is the quickest clue to what he or she thinks or feels. Your players know this, so they will study your face, looking for any sign that will tell them more than the words you say. Don't try to fool them by putting on a happy or blank "mask." They'll see through it, and you'll lose credibility.

Serious, stone-faced expressions are no help to kids who need cues that indicate how they are performing. They will just assume you're unhappy or disinterested. Don't be afraid to smile. A smile from a coach can give a great boost to an unsure young athlete. Plus, a smile lets your players know that you are happy coaching them. But don't overdo it, or your players won't be able to tell when you are genuinely pleased by something they've done or when you are just putting on a smiling face.

Body Language

What would your players think you were feeling if you came to practice slouched over, with head down and shoulders slumped?

Tired? Bored? Unhappy? What would they think you were feeling if you watched them during a match with your hands on your hips, your jaws clenched, and your face reddened? Upset with them? Disgusted at an official? Mad at a fan? Probably some or all of these things would enter your players' minds. And none of these impressions is the kind you want your players to have of you. That's why you should carry yourself in a pleasant, confident, and vigorous manner. Such a posture not only projects happiness with your coaching role but also provides a good example for your young players who may model your behavior.

Physical contact can also be a very important use of body language. A handshake, a pat on the back, an arm around the shoulder, or even a big hug are effective ways of showing approval, concern, affection, and joy to your players. Youngsters need this type of non-verbal message. Keep within the obvious moral and legal limits, but don't be reluctant to touch your players and send a message that can only truly be expressed in that way.

How Can I Improve My Receiving Skills?

Now, let's examine the other half of the communication process—receiving messages. Too often people are very good senders but very poor receivers of messages. As a coach of young athletes, it is essential that you are able to fulfill both roles effectively.

The requirements for receiving messages are quite simple, but receiving skills are perhaps less satisfying and therefore underdeveloped. People seem to naturally enjoy hearing themselves talk more than they enjoy hearing others. But if you are willing to read about the keys to receiving messages and to make a strong effort to use them with your players, you'll be surprised by what you've been missing.

Attention!

First, you must pay attention; you must want to hear what others have to communicate to you. That's not always easy when you're busy coaching and have many things competing for your attention. But

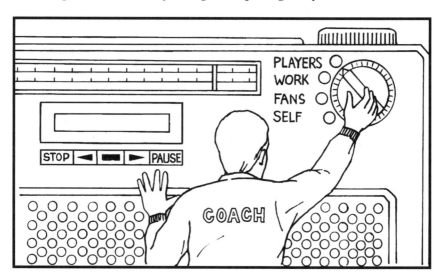

in one-to-one or team meetings with players, you must really focus on what they are telling you, both verbally and nonverbally. You'll be amazed at the little signals you pick up. Not only will such focused attention help you catch every word your players say, but you'll also notice your players' moods and physical states, and you'll get an idea of your players' feelings toward you and other players on the team.

Listen CARE-FULLY

How we receive messages from others, perhaps more than anything else we do, demonstrates how much we care for the sender and what that person has to tell us. If you care little for your players or have little regard for what they have to say, it will show in how you attend and listen to them. Check yourself. Do you find your mind wandering to what you are going to do after practice while one of your players is talking to you? Do you frequently have to ask your players, "What did you say?" If so, you need to work on your receiving mechanics of attending and listening. If you find that you're missing the messages your players send, perhaps the most critical question you should ask yourself is this: "Do I care?"

How Do I Put It All Together?

So far we've discussed separately the sending and receiving of messages. But we all know that senders and receivers switch roles several times during an interaction. One person initiates communication by sending a message to another person, who then receives the message. The receiver then switches roles and becomes the sender by responding to the person who sent the initial message. These verbal and nonverbal responses are called feedback.

Your players will be looking to you for feedback all the time. They will want to know how you think they are performing, what you think of their ideas, and whether their efforts please you. Obviously, you can respond in many different ways. How you respond will strongly affect your players. So let's take a look at a few general types of feedback and examine their possible effects.

Providing Instructions

With young players, much of your feedback will involve answering questions about how to play tennis. Your instructive responses to these questions should include both verbal and nonverbal feedback. Here are some suggestions for giving instructional feedback:

- Keep verbal instructions simple and concise.
- Use demonstrations to provide nonverbal instructional feedback (see unit 4).
- "Walk" players through the skill, or use a slow-motion demonstration if they are having trouble learning.

Correcting Errors

When your players perform incorrectly, you need to provide informative feedback to correct the error—and the sooner the better. When

you do correct errors, keep in mind these two principles: Use negative criticism sparingly, and keep calm.

Use Negative Criticism Sparingly

Although you may need to punish players for horseplay or dangerous activities by scolding or removing them from activity temporarily, avoid reprimanding players for performance errors. Admonishing players for honest mistakes makes them afraid to even try. Nothing ruins a youngster's enjoyment of a sport more than a coach who harps on every miscue. So instead, correct your players by using the positive approach. Your players will enjoy playing more, and you'll enjoy coaching more.

Keep Calm

Don't fly off the handle when your players make mistakes. Remember, you're coaching young and inexperienced players, not pros. You'll therefore see more incorrect than correct technique, and you'll probably have more discipline problems than you expect. But throwing a tantrum over each error or misbehavior will only inhibit your

players or suggest to them the wrong kind of behavior to model. So let your players know that mistakes aren't the end of the world; stay cool!

Giving Positive Feedback

Praising players when they have performed or behaved well is an effective way of getting them to repeat (or try to repeat) that behavior in the future. And positive feedback for effort is an especially effective way to motivate youngsters to work on difficult skills. So rather than shouting and providing negative feedback to a player who has made a mistake, try offering players a compliment sandwich, described on page 24.

Sometimes just the way you word feedback can make it more positive than negative. For example, instead of saying, "Don't

Coaches, be positive!

Only a very small percentage of ASEP-trained coaches' behaviors are negative.

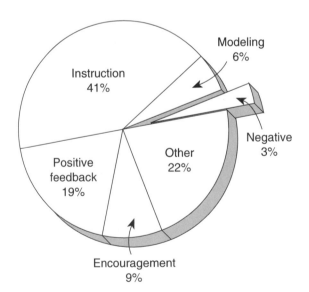

try to kill the ball," you might say, "Swing smoothly and with moderate force." Then your players will be focusing on what to do instead of what not to do.

You can give positive feedback verbally and nonverbally. Telling a player, especially in front of teammates, that he or she has performed well is a great way to boost the youngster's confidence. A pat on the back or a handshake can be a very tangible way of communicating your recognition of a player's performance.

Who Else Do I Need to Communicate With?

Coaching involves not only sending and receiving messages and providing proper feedback to players, but also interacting with parents, fans, officials, and opposing coaches. If you don't communicate effectively with these groups of people, your coaching career will be unpleasant and short-lived. So try the following suggestions for communicating with these groups.

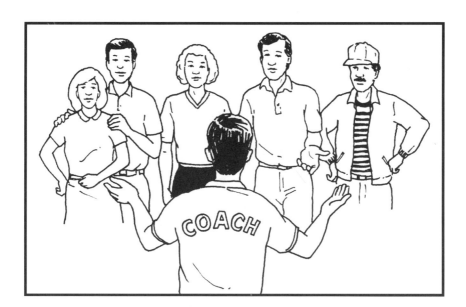

Parents

A player's parents need to be assured that their son or daughter is under the direction of a coach who is both knowledgeable about tennis and concerned about the youngster's well-being. You can put their worries to rest by holding a preseason parent orientation meeting in which you describe your background and your approach to coaching.

If parents contact you with a concern during the season, listen to them closely and try to offer positive responses. If you need to communicate with parents, catch them after a practice, give them a phone call, or send a note through the mail. Messages sent to parents through children are too often lost, misinterpreted, or forgotten.

Fans

The stands probably won't be overflowing at your matches, but that only means that you'll more easily hear the few fans who criticize your coaching. When you hear something negative said about the job you're doing, don't respond. Keep calm, consider whether the message has any value, and if not, forget it. Acknowledging critical, unwarranted comments from a fan during a game will only encourage others to voice their opinions. So put away your "rabbit ears" and communicate to fans, through your actions, that you are a confident, competent coach.

Even if you are ready to withstand the negative comments of fans, your players may not be. Prepare your players for fans' criticisms. Tell them it is you, not the spectators, to whom they should listen. If you notice that one of your players is rattled by a fan's comment, reassure the player that your evaluation is more objective and favorable—and the one that counts.

Officials

How you communicate with officials will have a great influence on the way your players behave toward them. Therefore, you need to set an example. Greet officials with a handshake, an introduction, and perhaps some casual conversation about the upcoming match. Indicate your respect for them before, during, and after the game. Don't make nasty remarks, shout, or use disrespectful body gestures. Your players will see you do it, and they'll get the idea that such behavior is appropriate. Plus, if the official hears or sees you, the communication between the two of you will break down.

Opposing Coaches

Make an effort to visit with the coach of the opposing team before the match. Perhaps the two of you can work out a special arrangement, such as matching up players of equal size and strength. During the match, don't get into a personal feud with the opposing coach. Remember, it's the kids, not the coaches, who are competing. And by getting along well with the opposing coach, you'll show your players that competition involves cooperation.

✔ *Summary Checklist*

Now, check your coach-communication skills by answering "Yes" or "No" to the following questions.

	Yes	No
1. Are your verbal messages to your players positive and honest?	___	___
2. Do you speak loudly, clearly, and in a language your athletes understand?	___	___
3. Do you remember to repeat instructions to your players, in case they didn't hear you the first time?	___	___
4. Are the tone of your voice and your nonverbal messages consistent with the words you use?	___	___
5. Do your facial expressions and body language express interest in and happiness with your coaching role?	___	___
6. Are you attentive to your players and able to pick up even their small verbal and nonverbal cues?	___	___
7. Do you really care about what your athletes say to you?	___	___
8. Do you instruct rather than criticize when your players make errors?	___	___
9. Are you usually positive when responding to things your athletes say and do?	___	___
10. Do you try to communicate in a cooperative and respectful manner with players' parents, fans, officials, and opposing coaches?	___	___

If you answered "No" to any of the above questions, you may want to refer back to the section of the chapter where the topic was discussed. The time to address communication problems is now, not when you're coaching your players.

Unit 4

How Do I Get My Players Ready for Matches?

To coach tennis, you must understand the basic rules, skills, and strategies. The second part of this book provides the basic information you'll need to comprehend the sport.

But all the tennis knowledge in the world will do you little good unless you present it effectively to your players. That's why this unit is so important. Here you will learn the steps to take when teaching sport skills, as well as practical guidelines for planning your season and individual practices.

How Do I Teach Tennis Skills?

Many people believe that the only qualification needed to coach is to have played the sport. It's helpful to have played, but there is much more to coaching successfully. Even if you haven't played or even watched tennis, you can still learn to coach successfully with this IDEA:

I—Introduce the skill.

D—Demonstrate the skill.

E—Explain the skill.

A—Attend to players practicing the skill.

Introduce the Skill

Players, especially young and inexperienced ones, need to know what skill they are learning and why they are learning it. You should therefore take these three steps every time you introduce a skill to your players:

1. Get your players' attention.

2. Name the skill.

3. Explain the importance of the skill.

Get Your Players' Attention

Because youngsters are easily distracted, use some method to get their attention. Some coaches use interesting news items or stories. Others use jokes. And others simply project enthusiasm that gets their players to listen. Whatever method you use, speak slightly above the normal volume and look your players in the eyes when you speak.

Also, position players so they can see and hear you. Arrange the players in two or three evenly spaced rows, facing you and not the sun or some source of distraction. Then ask if everyone can see and hear you before you begin.

Name the Skill

Although you might mention other common names for the skill, decide which one you'll use and stick with it. This will help avoid confusion and enhance communication among your players. For example, choose either "serve" or "service" as the term you'll use, then use it exclusively.

Explain the Importance of the Skill

Although the importance of a skill may be apparent to you, your players may be less able to see how the skill will help them become better players. Offer them a reason for learning the skill and describe how the skill relates to more advanced skills.

> "The most difficult aspect of coaching is this: Coaches must learn to let athletes learn. Sport skills should be taught so they have meaning to the child, not just meaning to the coach."
>
> Rainer Martens, ASEP Founder

Demonstrate the Skill

The demonstration step is the most important part of teaching a skill to young players who may have never done anything closely resembling it. They need a picture, not just words. They need to see how the skill is performed.

If you are unable to perform the skill correctly, have an assistant coach or someone skilled in it perform the demonstration. A high school varsity player would be an excellent choice. These tips will help make your demonstrations more effective:

- Use correct form.
- Demonstrate the skill several times.
- Slow down the skill, if possible, during one or two performances so players can see every movement involved.
- Perform the skill at different angles so your players can get a full perspective of it.
- Demonstrate the skill from both the right and left sides.

Explain the Skill

Players learn more effectively when they're given a brief explanation of the skill along with the demonstration. Use simple terms to describe the skill and, if possible, relate it to previously learned skills. Ask your players whether they understand your description. A good technique is to ask the team to repeat your explanation. Ask questions like, "What are you going to do first?" and "Then what?" Watch for looks of confusion or uncertainty and repeat your explanation and demonstration of those points. If possible, use different words so that your players get a chance to try to understand from a different perspective.

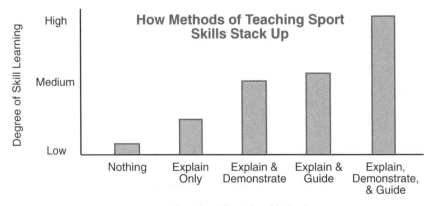

Coaches' Teaching Methods

Complex skills often are better understood when they are explained in more manageable parts. For instance, if you want to teach your players how to hit a lob to deep along the baseline, you might take the following steps:

1. Show them a correct performance of the entire skill and explain its function.
2. Break down the skill and point out its component parts to your players.
3. Have players perform each of the component skills you have already taught them, such as getting to the ball, identifying where to hit the ball, and using the proper racket angle when contacting the ball.
4. After players have demonstrated their ability to perform the separate parts of the skill in sequence, reexplain the entire skill.
5. Have players practice the skill.

One caution: Young players have short attention spans, and a long demonstration or explanation of the skill will bore them. So spend no more than a few minutes combined on the introduction, demonstration, and explanation phases. Then get the players active in attempts to perform the skill. The total IDEA should be completed in 10 minutes or less, followed by individual and group practice activities.

Attend to Players Practicing the Skill

If the skill you selected was within your players' capabilities, and you have done an effective job of introducing, demonstrating, and explaining it, your players should be ready to attempt the skill. Some players may need to be physically guided through the movements during their first few attempts. For example, some players may need your hands-on help to get their feet in the correct position for the lob. Walking unsure athletes through the skill in this way will help them gain confidence to perform the skill on their own.

Your teaching duties don't end when all your athletes have demonstrated that they understand how to perform the skill. In fact, a significant part of your teaching will involve observing closely the hit-and-miss trial performances of your players.

As you observe players' efforts in drills and activities, offer positive, corrective feedback in the form of the compliment sandwich described in unit 3. If a player performs the skill properly, acknowledge it and offer praise. Keep in mind that your feedback will have a great influence on your players' motivation to practice and improve their performance.

Remember, too, that young players need individual instruction. So set aside a time before, during, or after practice to give individual help.

What Planning Do I Need to Do?

Beginning coaches often make the mistake of showing up for the first practice with no particular plan in mind. These coaches find that their practices are unorganized, their players are frustrated and inattentive, and the amount and quality of their skill instruction is limited. Planning is essential to successful teaching and coaching. And it doesn't begin on the way to practice!

Preseason Planning

Effective coaches begin planning well before the start of the season. Among the preseason measures that will make the season more enjoyable, successful, and safe for you and your players are the following:

- Familiarize yourself with the sport organization you are involved in, especially its philosophy and goals regarding youth sport.
- Examine the availability of facilities, equipment, instructional aids, and other materials needed for practices and meets.
- Find out what fund-raising you and your players will be expected to do, and decide on the best way to meet your goals.
- Make arrangements for any team travel that will be required during the season. Consider clearance forms, supervision, transportation, equipment, contacting parents, and safety.
- Check to see whether you have adequate liability insurance to cover you if one of your players gets hurt (see unit 5). If you don't, get some.
- Establish your coaching priorities regarding having fun, developing players' skills, and winning.
- Select and meet with your assistant coaches to discuss the philosophy, goals, team rules, and plans for the season.

- Register players for the team. Have them complete a player information form and obtain medical clearance forms, if required.
- Institute an injury-prevention program for your players.
- Hold an orientation meeting to inform parents of your background, philosophy, goals, and instructional approach. Also, give a brief overview of the league's rules, terms, and strategies to familiarize parents or guardians with the sport.

You may be surprised at the number of things you should do even before the first practice. But if you address them during the preseason, the season will be much more enjoyable and productive for you and your players.

In-Season Planning

Your choice of activities during the season should be based on whether they will help your players develop physical and mental skills, knowledge of rules and game tactics, sportsmanship, and love for the sport. All of these goals are important, but we'll focus on tennis skills and tactics to give you an idea of how to itemize your objectives.

Goal Setting

What you plan to do during the season must be reasonable for the maturity and skill level of your players. In terms of tennis skills and tactics, you should teach young players the basics and move on to more complex activities only after the players have mastered these easier techniques and strategies.

To begin the season, your instructional goals might include the following:

- Players will be able to get into a correct stance for any shot they might make or play.
- Players will be able to use proper footwork for various types of shots.

- Players will be able to demonstrate correct positioning for effective returns of serve.
- Players will be able to demonstrate proper forehand and backhand techniques.
- Players will be able to demonstrate knowledge of tennis rules.
- Players will be able to demonstrate teamwork throughout the season.
- Players will be able to demonstrate their preparation for practices and matches during those events.
- Players will be able to demonstrate a basic understanding of offensive and defensive strategies.
- Players will be able to demonstrate good sportsmanship at all times.
- Players will increase their enjoyment of tennis and develop an interest in learning more about the game.

Organizing

After you've defined the skills and tactics you want your players to learn during the season, you can plan how to teach them to your players in practices. But be flexible! If your players are having difficulty learning a skill or tactic, take some extra time until they get the hang of it—even if that means moving back your schedule. After all, if your players are unable to perform the fundamental skills, they'll never execute the more complex skills you have scheduled for them, and they won't have much fun trying. It also helps to have a plan for progressing players through skills during the season.

The way you organize your season may also help your players to develop socially and psychologically. By giving your players responsibility for certain aspects of practices—leading warm-up and stretching activities are common examples—you help players to develop self-esteem and take responsibility for themselves and the team. As you plan your season, consider ways to provide your players with experiences that lead them to steadily improve these skills.

What Makes a Good Practice?

A good instructional plan makes practice preparation much easier. Have players work on more important and less difficult goals in early-season practice sessions. And see to it that players master basic skills before moving on to more advanced ones.

It is helpful to establish one goal for each practice, but try to include a variety of activities related to that goal. For example, although your primary objective might be to improve players' serving ability, you should have players perform several different drills designed to enhance that single skill. To add more variety to your practices, vary the order of the activities you schedule for players to perform.

In general, we recommend that in each of your practices you do the following:

- *Warm up.*
- *Practice previously taught skills.*
- *Teach and practice new skills.*
- *Practice under competitive conditions.*
- *Cool down.*
- *Evaluate.*

Warm Up

As you're checking the roster and announcing the performance goals for the practice, your players should be preparing their bodies for vigorous activity. A 5- to 10-minute period of easy-paced activities (three-quarter-speed running around the courts), stretching, and calisthenics should be sufficient for youngsters to limber their muscles and reduce the risk of injury.

Practice Previously Taught Skills

Devote part of each practice to having players work on the fundamental skills they already know. But remember, kids like variety. Thus you should organize and modify drills so that everyone is involved and stays interested. Praise and encourage players when you notice improvement, and offer individual assistance to those who need help.

Teach and Practice New Skills

Gradually build on your players' existing skills by giving players something new to practice each session. The proper method for teaching sport skills is described on pages 38–42. Refer to those pages if you have any questions about teaching new skills or if you want to evaluate your teaching approach periodically during the season.

Practice Under Competitive Conditions

Competition among teammates during practices prepares players for actual games and informs young athletes about their abilities relative to their peers. Youngsters also seem to have more fun in competitive activities.

You can create game-like conditions by using competitive drills, modified games, and scrimmages (see units 7 and 8). However, consider the following guidelines before introducing competition into your practices:

- All players should have an equal opportunity to participate.
- Match players by ability and physical maturity.
- Make sure that players can execute fundamental skills before they compete in groups.
- Emphasize performing well, not winning, in every competition.
- Give players room to make mistakes by avoiding constant evaluation of their performances.

Cool Down

Each practice should wind down with a 5- to 10-minute period of light exercise, including jogging, performance of simple skills, and some stretching. The cool-down allows athletes' bodies to return to the resting state and avoid stiffness, and it affords you an opportunity to review the practice.

Evaluate

At the end of practice spend a few minutes with your players reviewing how well the session accomplished the goals you had set. Even if your evaluation is negative, show optimism for future practices and send players off on an upbeat note.

How Do I Put a Practice Together?

Simply knowing the six practice components is not enough. You must also be able to arrange those components into a logical progression and fit them into a time schedule. Now, using your instructional goals as a guide for selecting what skills to have your players work on, try to plan several practices you might conduct. The following examples should help you get started.

Sample Practice Plan

Performance Objective. Players will be able to hit full-swing serves from the baseline.

Component	Time	Activity or drill
Warm-up	8 min	Groundstroke & Dig followed by selected stretches
Teach	12 min	Serve Progression
Practice previously learned skills	20 min	Serve Practice, Serve and Return
Practice under match-like conditions	10 min	Team Singles
Evaluation and cool-down	10 min	Ball Reaction drill, stretching

✔ *Summary Checklist*

During your tennis season, check your planning and teaching skills periodically. As you gain more coaching experience, you should be able to answer "Yes" to each of the following.

When you plan, do you remember to plan for

_____ preseason events such as player registration, fund-raising, travel, liability protection, use of facilities, and parent orientation?

_____ season goals such as the development of players' physical skills, mental skills, sportsmanship, and enjoyment?

_____ practice components such as warm-up, practicing previously taught skills, teaching and practicing new skills, practicing under competitive conditions, cool-down, and evaluation?

When you teach skills to your players, do you

_____ arrange the players so all can see and hear?

_____ introduce the skill clearly and explain its importance?

_____ demonstrate the skill properly several times?

_____ explain the skill simply and accurately?

_____ attend closely to players practicing the skill?

_____ offer corrective, positive feedback or praise after observing players' attempts at the skill?

Unit 5

What About Safety?

Your best singles player smashes an overhead winner but slumps to the court. She writhes in pain while gripping her left ankle. What do you do?

No coach wants to see players get hurt. But injury remains a reality of sport participation; consequently, you must be prepared to provide first aid when injuries occur and to protect yourself against unjustified lawsuits. Fortunately, there are many preventive measures coaches can institute to reduce the risk. This unit will describe how you can

- create the safest possible environment for your players,
- provide emergency first aid to players when they get hurt, and
- protect yourself from injury liability.

How Do I Keep My Players From Getting Hurt?

Injuries may occur because of poor preventive measures. Part of your planning, described in unit 4, should include steps that give your players the best possible chance for injury-free participation. These steps include the following:

- *Preseason physical examination*
- *Nutrition*
- *Physical conditioning*
- *Equipment and facilities inspection*
- *Matching athletes by physical maturity and warning of inherent risks*
- *Proper supervision and record keeping*
- *Providing water breaks*
- *Warm-up and cool-down*

Preseason Physical Examination

In the absence of severe injury or ongoing illness, your players should have a physical examination every 2 years. If a player has a known complication, a physician's consent should be obtained before participation is allowed. You should also have players' parents or guardians sign a participation agreement form and a release form to allow their children to be treated in case of an emergency.

INFORMED CONSENT FORM

I hereby give my permission for _____ to participate

in _____ during the athletic season beginning in _____ (year). Further, I authorize the school to provide emergency treatment of an injury to or illness of my child if qualified medical personnel consider treatment necessary *and* perform the treatment. This authorization is granted only if I cannot be reached and a reasonable effort has been made to do so.

Date _____ Parent or guardian _____

Address _____ Phone ( ) _____

Family physician _____ Phone ( ) _____

Pre-existing medical conditions (e.g., allergies or chronic illnesses) _____

_____

Other(s) to also contact in case of emergency _____

Relationship to child _____ Phone ( ) _____

My child and I are aware that participating in _____ is a potentially hazardous activity. I assume all risks associated with participation in this sport, including but not limited to falls, contact with other participants, the effects of the weather, traffic, and other reasonable risk conditions associated with the sport. All such risks to my child are known and understood by me.

I understand this informed consent form and agree to its conditions on behalf of my child.

Child's signature _____ Date _____

Parent's signature _____ Date _____

Nutrition

Increasingly, disordered eating and unhealthy dietary habits are affecting youth tennis players. Let players and parents know the importance of healthy eating and the dangers that can arise from efforts to lose weight too quickly. Young tennis players need to supply their bodies with the extra energy they need to keep up with the demands of practices and matches. Ask your director about information that you can pass on to your players and their parents, and include a discussion of basic, commonsense nutrition in your parent orientation meeting.

Physical Conditioning

Muscles, tendons, and ligaments unaccustomed to vigorous and long-lasting physical activity are prone to injury. Therefore, prepare your athletes to withstand the exertion of playing tennis. An effective conditioning program would involve running sprints and strength training.

Make conditioning drills and activities fun. Include a skill component, such as firing out of a stance, to prevent players from becoming bored or looking upon the activity as work. A serve-and-return game or forehand progression drill would be a good drill to add for young players to develop their skills and make the practices fun and exciting.

Keep in mind, too, that players on your team may respond differently to conditioning activities. Wide-ranging levels of fitness or natural ability might mean that an activity that challenges one child is beyond another's ability to complete safely. The environment is another factor that may affect players' responses to activity. The same workout that was effective on a cool morning might be hazardous to players on a hot, humid afternoon. Similarly, an activity children excel in at sea level might present a risk at higher altitudes. An ideal conditioning program prepares players for the season's demands without neglecting physical and environmental factors that affect their safety.

Equipment and Facilities Inspection

Another way to prevent injuries is to check the quality of the racket and the quality and fit of the clothes and shoes used by your players.

Slick-soled, poor fitting, or loosely laced shoes are a knee or ankle injury waiting to happen. Make sure your players' shoes are appropriate for the surfaces on which they play, are the proper size for their feet, and are double-tied to prevent self-inflicted "shoestring stumbles." Two pairs of socks are better than one for preventing blisters.

Check the quality of all equipment and uniforms before fitting them to the kids on your team. After distributing good equipment, show players how to take care of it.

Remember, also, to examine regularly the courts on which your players practice and play. Remove hazards, report conditions you cannot remedy, and request maintenance as necessary. If unsafe conditions exist, either make adaptations to avoid risk to your players' safety or stop the practice or match until safe conditions have been restored.

Matching Athletes by Physical Maturity and Warning of Inherent Risks

Children of the same age may differ in height and weight by up to 6 inches and 50 pounds. In tennis , the advantage of size and maturity is critical. It is not fair or safe to pit an underdeveloped young athlete against a player whose physique belongs in the U.S. Open.

Try to give smaller, less mature children a better chance to succeed and avoid injury, and larger children more of a challenge. Experience, ability, and emotional maturity are additional factors to keep in mind when matching players on the court.

Matching helps protect you from certain liability concerns. But you also must warn players of the inherent risks involved in playing tennis, because "failure to warn" is one of the most successful arguments in lawsuits against coaches. So, thoroughly explain the inherent risks of tennis, and make sure each player knows, understands, and appreciates those risks.

The preseason parent orientation meeting is a good opportunity to explain the risks of tennis to parents and players. It is also a good occasion on which to have the players and their parents sign waivers releasing you from liability should an injury occur. Such waivers do not relieve you of responsibility for your players' well-being, but they are recommended by lawyers.

Proper Supervision and Record Keeping

When you work with youngsters, your mere presence in the area of play is not enough; you must actively plan and direct team activities and closely observe and evaluate players' participation. You're the watchdog responsible for the players' well-being. So if you notice a player limping or grimacing, give him or her a rest and examine the extent of the injury.

As a coach, you're also required to enforce the rules of the sport, prohibit dangerous horseplay, and hold practices and meets only under safe weather conditions. These specific supervisory activities will make the play environment safer for your players and will help protect you from liability if a mishap does occur.

For further protection, keep records of your season plans, practice plans, and players' injuries. Season and practice plans come in handy when you need evidence that players have been taught certain skills, whereas accurate, detailed accident report forms offer protection against unfounded lawsuits. Ask for these forms from the organization to which you belong. And hold on to these records for several years so that an "old tennis injury" of a former player doesn't come back to haunt you.

Providing Water Breaks

Tennis is an extremely vigorous aerobic activity. You know how hot and humid it can get out on a tennis court. And if you add to that a lot of activity and competition, body temperatures can really rise. Encourage players to drink plenty of water before, during, and after practices and matches. Because water makes up 45% to 65% of a youngster's body weight and water weighs about a pound per pint, the loss of even a little water can have severe consequences for the body's systems. And it doesn't have to be hot and humid for players to become dehydrated. Nor do players have to feel thirsty; in fact, by the time they are aware of their thirst, they are long overdue for a drink.

Warm-Up and Cool-Down

Although young bodies are generally very limber, they, too, can get tight from inactivity. Therefore, a warm-up period of approximately 10 minutes before each practice is strongly recommended. The warm-up should address each muscle group and get the heart rate elevated in preparation for strenuous activity. Easy running followed by these stretching exercises is a common sequence (hold each stretch for 20 seconds, then release):

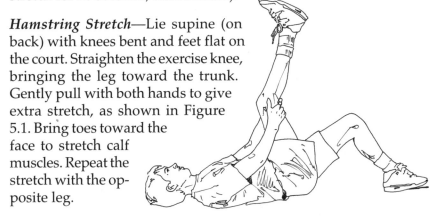

Hamstring Stretch—Lie supine (on back) with knees bent and feet flat on the court. Straighten the exercise knee, bringing the leg toward the trunk. Gently pull with both hands to give extra stretch, as shown in Figure 5.1. Bring toes toward the face to stretch calf muscles. Repeat the stretch with the opposite leg.

■ **Figure 5.1** Hamstring stretch.

Hip Twist—Lie supine (on back) with knees bent, feet flat on the court, hands clasped behind the head, and arms resting on the court. Place the left ankle outside the right knee. Use the left leg to pull the right knee toward the floor, as shown in Figure 5.2. Keep the upper back, head, shoulders, and elbows flat on the court. Move slowly and *do not* rock from side to side. Switch legs and repeat the stretch.

■ **Figure 5.2**   Hip twist.

Long-Sitting Stretch—Sit on the court with both legs straight, toes pointing toward your face, and hands resting on the thighs. Lean forward over both legs, bringing the chest toward the thighs, as shown in Figure 5.3. Keep looking straight ahead but do not reach for the toes.

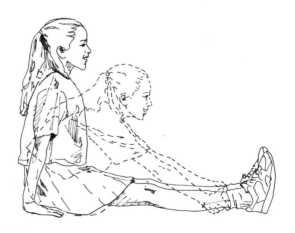

■ **Figure 5.3**   Long-sitting stretch.

Groin Stretch—Stand with legs as far apart as possible without being painful and keep abdominal muscles firm. Place the left hand on the left knee and the right hand on the right hip. Slowly bend the left knee until the right thigh is nearly parallel to the court (Figure 5.4). Roll onto the inner side of the right foot while keeping the foot on the floor during the stretch. Repeat the stretch in the opposite direction.

■ **Figure 5.4** Groin stretch.

Stork Stretch—Stand on the left leg, holding onto the fence or net with the left hand for balance. Bend the right knee and grasp the right ankle with the right hand (knee will be pointing forward). Roll the pelvis under so that the back is flat. Keeping the lower back flat and buttocks tucked under, bring the right knee down as far as possible, trying to point the knee straight down to the court, as shown in Figure 5.5. Repeat the stretch with the opposite leg.

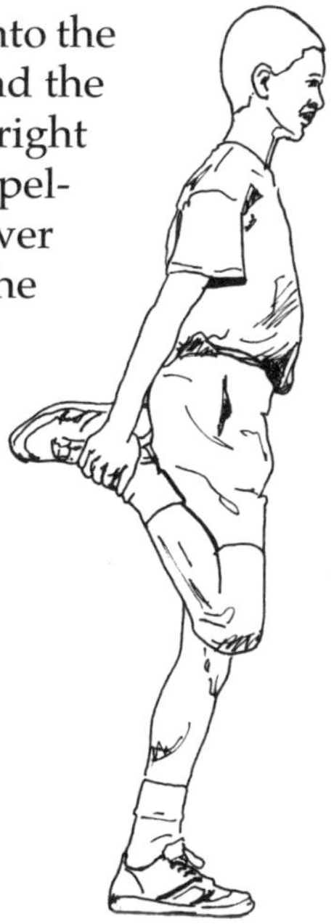

■ **Figure 5.5** Stork stretch.

Fence Stretch—Stand facing the fence with the left leg behind the right. Place both hands against the fence for balance, as shown in Figure 5.6a. Keep the body in a straight line throughout the exercise, and do not let the left foot rotate outward. Holding the left knee straight and keeping the left heel flat on the court, bend the right knee while leaning the trunk forward (Figure 5.6a) to feel the stretch in the calf. Do not arch the lower back. To feel the stretch in the left heel, slightly bend the left knee and raise the left heel about 2 inches off the court (Figure 5.6b). The left foot must be pointing forward throughout the exercise. Repeat the stretch for the right leg.

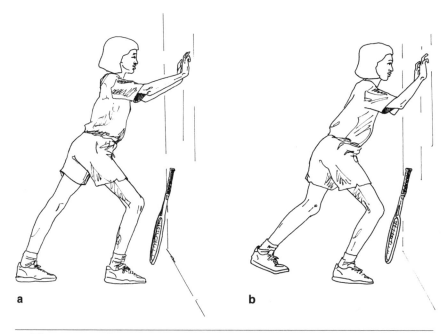

a   b

■ **Figure 5.6** Fence stretch.

Arm Hang—Stand facing the fence with the knees slightly bent. Hold onto the fence with hands about shoulder-width apart and let the body drop down, as shown in Figure 5.7.

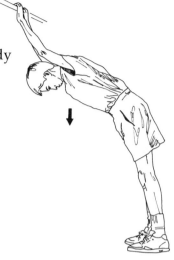

■ **Figure 5.7** Arm hang.

Racket Stretch—Hold the racket in the left hand, drape it over the left shoulder, and grasp it from behind the back with the right hand. Slowly pull down, stretching the left arm. Then pull up, stretching the right arm (see Figure 5.8). Switch arms and repeat the exercise.

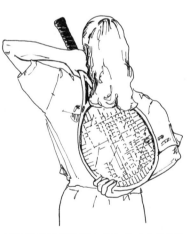

■ **Figure 5.8** Racket stretch.

Forearm Stretch—Stand holding the right arm in front of the body with the elbow completely straight and the palm down. Use the left hand to slowly stretch the wrist back, as shown in Figure 5.9a. Next, slowly stretch the right wrist down, as shown in Figure 5.9b. Turn the right palm up and repeat the first two stretches, then repeat the exercise for the left wrist.

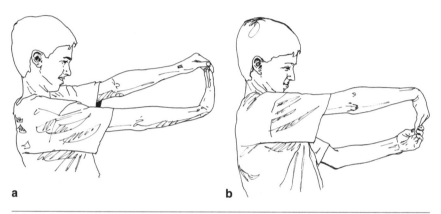

a   b

■ **Figure 5.9** Forearm stretch.

Neck Semicircles—Standing with the head bent to the right (right ear toward the right shoulder), make a half-circle with the neck going forward (chin to chest), then bring the left ear toward the left shoulder. Next, bring the head to a neutral position and turn to look over the right shoulder as far as possible. Then turn to look over the left shoulder as far as possible.

As practice is winding down, slow players' heart rates with some moderate then easy-paced activities. Continuous, half-speed execution of all your groundstrokes can be a good way to cool down and review simultaneously. Before you call it a day, arrange for a 5- to 10-minute period of easy stretching at the end of practice to help players avoid stiff muscles and make them less tight before the next practice.

What if One of My Players Gets Hurt?

No matter how good and thorough your prevention program, injuries will occur. When injury does strike, chances are you will be the one in charge. The severity and nature of the injury will determine how actively involved you'll be in treating the injury. But regardless of how seriously a player is hurt, it is your responsibility to know what steps to take. So let's look at how you can provide basic emergency care to your injured athletes.

Minor Injuries

Although no injury seems minor to the person experiencing it, most injuries are neither life threatening nor severe enough to restrict participation. When such injuries occur, you can take an active role in their initial treatment.

ASEP Fact

You shouldn't let a fear of acquired immune deficiency syndrome (AIDS) stop you from helping a player. On the field you are only at risk if you allow contaminated blood to come in contact with an open wound, so the blood barrier that you wear will protect you from AIDS should one of your players carry this disease. Check with your director or ASEP for more information about protecting yourself and your participants from AIDS.

Scrapes and Cuts

When one of your players has an open wound, the first thing you should do is to put on a pair of disposable surgical gloves or some other effective blood barrier. Then follow these four steps:

1. Stop the bleeding by applying direct pressure with a clean dressing to the wound and elevating it. The player may be able to apply this pressure while you put on your gloves. Do not remove the dressing if it becomes soaked with blood. Instead, place an additional dressing on top of the one already in place. If bleeding continues, elevate the injured area above the heart and maintain pressure.

2. Cleanse the wound thoroughly once the bleeding is controlled. A good rinsing with a forceful stream of water, and perhaps light scrubbing with soap, will help prevent infection.

3. <u>Protect the wound</u> with sterile gauze or a bandage. If the player continues to participate, apply protective padding over the injured area.

4. <u>Remove and dispose of gloves</u> carefully to prevent you or anyone else from coming into contact with blood.

For bloody noses not associated with serious facial injury, have the athlete sit and lean slightly forward. Then pinch the player's nostrils shut. If the bleeding continues after several minutes, or if the athlete has a history of nosebleeds, seek medical assistance.

Strains and Sprains

The physical demands of tennis practices and matches often result in injury to the muscles or tendons (strains), or to the ligaments (sprains). When your players suffer minor strains or sprains, immediately apply the PRICE method of injury care.

Bumps and Bruises

At times, tennis players dive or fall to the ground. If the force of a body part at impact is great enough, a bump or bruise will result. Many players continue playing with such sore spots, but if the bump or bruise is large and painful, you should act appropriately. Enact the PRICE method for injury care and monitor the injury. If swelling, discoloration, and pain have lessened, the player may resume participation with protective padding; if not, the player should be examined by a physician.

Serious Injuries

Head, neck, and back injuries; fractures; and injuries that cause a player to lose consciousness are among a class of injuries that you cannot, and should not, try to treat yourself. But you should plan for what you'll do if such an injury occurs. Your plan should include the following guidelines for action:

- Obtain the phone number and ensure the availability of nearby emergency care units. Include this information as part of a written emergency plan before the season, and have it with you at every practice and meet.

The PRICE Method

P—Protect the athlete and injured body part from further danger or further trauma.

R—Rest the area to avoid further damage and foster healing.

I—Ice the area to reduce swelling and pain.

C—Compress the area by securing an ice bag in place with an elastic wrap.

E—Elevate the injury above heart level to keep the blood from pooling in the area.

- Assign an assistant coach or another adult the responsibility of knowing the location of the nearest phone and contacting emergency medical help upon your request.
- Ensure that emergency medical information, treatment, and transportation consent forms are available during every practice and meet.
- Do not move the injured athlete.
- Calm the injured athlete and keep others away from him or her as much as possible.
- Evaluate whether the athlete's breathing is stopped or irregular, and if necessary, clear the airway with your fingers.
- Administer artificial respiration if breathing is stopped. Administer cardiopulmonary resuscitation (CPR), or have a trained individual administer CPR if the athlete's circulation has stopped.
- Remain with the athlete until medical personnel arrive.

How Do I Protect Myself?

When one of your players is injured, naturally your first concern is his or her well-being. Your feelings for children, after all, are what made you decide to coach. Unfortunately, there is something else that you must consider: Can you be held liable for the injury?

From a legal standpoint, a coach has nine duties to fulfill. We've discussed all but planning (see unit 4) in this unit:

1. Provide a safe environment.

2. Properly plan the activity.

3. Provide adequate and proper equipment.

4. Match or equate athletes.

5. Warn of inherent risks in the sport.

6. Supervise the activity closely.

7. Evaluate athletes for injury or incapacitation.

8. Know emergency procedures and first aid.

9. Keep adequate records.

In addition to fulfilling these nine legal duties, you should check your insurance coverage to make sure your policy will protect you from liability.

Summary Self-Test

Now that you've read how to make your coaching experience safe for your players and yourself, test your knowledge of the material by answering these questions:

1. What are eight injury-prevention measures you can institute to try to keep your players from getting hurt?
2. What is the four-step emergency care process for cuts?
3. What method of treatment is best for minor sprains and strains?
4. What steps can you take to manage serious injuries?
5. What are the nine legal duties of a coach?

What Is Tennis All About?

From reading the first part of this manual you've gotten a good general understanding of what it takes to coach. Now it's time to develop your comprehension of the rules of the game.

What Are the Rules?

Tennis is played worldwide in accordance with the official rules established by the International Tennis Federation (ITF). The USTA adheres to those rules plus The Code. The Code consists of the "unwritten" rules of tennis, which custom and tradition dictate that players follow in unofficiated matches. The rules and The Code apply to both *singles* and *doubles* play.

The Tennis Court

Before you teach players the rules of singles and doubles, make sure that they are familiar with all the lines of a tennis court. If you have any doubt about what each line represents, refer to Figure 6.1. Then instruct and quiz your players to ensure that they know what all the court markings mean.

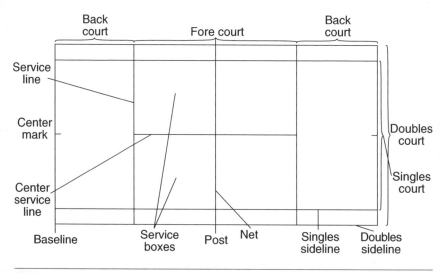

■ **Figure 6.1**   Tennis court.

Singles Play

One-on-one tennis is played on the singles court and requires each player to have a basic repertoire of skills to be successful. More basic than that, however, each player must understand the guidelines for participating in a singles match.

Serving

Tennis points begin with one player, called the *server*, hitting the ball from behind the baseline over the net into the receiver's service box. To see who serves first, players will spin a racket or toss a coin (see Figure 6.2). The player who wins the spin or toss may choose or make the opponent choose to *serve* first, receive first, or pick an end of the court on which to start the match.

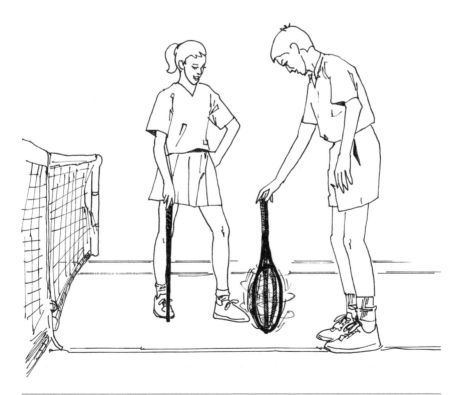

■ **Figure 6.2** Spinning the racket for first service.

Here are some instructions to give players about serving:

1. Before serving, be sure that the *receiver* is ready to play.

2. When serving the first point, you must stand behind the baseline between the center mark and the right singles sideline. Remember, you cannot step on or over the baseline until after you've hit the ball.

3. Your first serve must go over the net into the receiver's service court. If the first serve does not go into the correct court, it is called a *fault*. A second fault, or *double fault*, results in a point being awarded to the receiver.

4. If you serve a ball that hits the top of the net before bouncing into the correct service court, it's called a *let* (see Figure 6.3). The server serves again, with no penalty. If your serve hits the net and then goes outside the service court, it is ruled a fault.

5. When serving the next point, you'll switch to a position behind the baseline between the center mark and the left sideline. You must then serve the ball into the receiver's left service court.

■ **Figure 6.3** Service let.

Have players switch ends of the court at the conclusion of the first game. The player who served the previous game will receive serve throughout the next game. Players should switch ends again after the third, fifth, and every following odd-numbered game.

Playing a Point

The serve is only the starting point in tennis. You must also teach players how to perform after the serve. Except when serving, a player may stand anywhere—in or out of the court—on her or his side of the net. Players also have the choice of hitting the ball before it bounces or after one bounce, but the receiver must let the serve bounce once before hitting it.

The ball is still in play if it happens to touch the net or post. And players should continue the point when a ball lands on a boundary line of the court.

A player wins the point if he or she hits the ball over the net into the court on the other side and the opponent does not return it. A player loses the point if she or he hits the ball into the net or out of the court (unless the opponent volleys the outgoing ball). A player also loses the point if the ball touches his or her clothing, if the racket touches the net or post, if the ball is hit before it passes the net, or if the ball is deliberately hit more than once. Players are on their honor to make these calls against themselves.

Scoring

When players are ready to begin playing games, they'll need to know how to score. Here is a point-by-point scoring protocol that you can teach your players. Before long, the scoring system will become second nature to them.

1. The first point won by a player is *15*; the player with no points has *Love*.

2. If the next point is won by the same player, the score is *30-Love*.

3. If that player then wins the 3rd and 4th points, the score is *40-Love* and finally *game*.

4. If any of the points is won by the opposing player, the scoring may be 15-Love, 15-all, 15-30, 30-all, 30-40, or game (with the opponent being the game winner).

5. If each player wins 3 points to tie the game at 40-40, the score is called *deuce*. The player who wins the next point has the advantage, often called *ad in* for the server and *ad out* for the receiver. If the player with the advantage wins the next point, she or he wins the game; if not, the score goes back to deuce. Then the first player to score 2 points in a row after deuce wins the game.

6. Players must call the score of the set (such as 4-3) before they serve for the first point of the game. They must also call the game score just before serving for each point, as in Figure 6.4. The server's score is always said first.

7. The first player to win at least six games and to be ahead by at least two games wins a *set*. The first one to win two sets wins the *match*. If the score reaches six games all, players may play a *tie-break game* ("tie breaker"). Whoever wins this game wins the set.

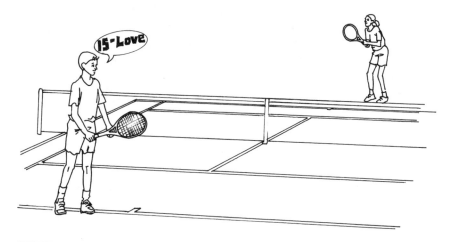

■ **Figure 6.4** Calling out the score before serving.

12-Point Tie-Break Game. If announced in advance of the match, a tie-break game may be used when the score reaches six games all in any set. The player (or doubles team) who first wins 7 points wins the game and the set provided he or she leads by a margin of 2 points. If the score reaches 6 points all, the game is extended until this margin has been achieved. Numerical scoring (1, 2, 3, etc.) is used throughout the tie-break game.

The player whose turn it is to serve is the server for the first point; the opponent is the server for the 2nd and 3rd points; and, thereafter, each player serves alternately for 2 consecutive points until the winner of the game and set has been decided.

Starting with the first point, serves are delivered alternately from the right and left courts, beginning from the right. The first server serves the first point from the right court; the second server serves the 2nd and 3rd points from the left and right courts, respectively; and so on.

Players change ends after every 6 points and at the conclusion of the tie-break game. The player (or doubles team) who served first in the tie-break game should receive serve in the first game of the following set.

9-Point Tie-Break Game. The 9-point tie-break game is sometimes used in sets played under *no-ad* scoring. The player who first wins 5 points wins the game and set. Numerical scoring (1, 2, 3, etc.) is used throughout the tie-break game.

In singles, the player whose turn it is to serve is the server for the first and 2nd points, into the right service court and then the left service court; the opponent is the server for the 3rd and 4th points, right and left. Players change ends.

The first server serves the 5th and 6th points, right and left; the opponent serves the 7th and 8th points, right and left. If the score reaches 4 points all, the second server serves the final point of the tie-break game into either the right or left court, whichever the opponent chooses.

In doubles, each player serves from the same end of the court that she or he served from during the set. The players stay on the same ends for one game of the next set, with the player (or doubles team) who served second in the tie-break game now serving first.

Calling Lines

Players share the responsibility for making loud, sure, and honest line calls. Unless the opponent asks for help, they may make calls only on their own side of the net. The following are guidelines you should set for your players to help them make proper line calls:

- If the ball touches any part of the line, it is good. Call the ball *out* only if you can clearly see a space between where the ball lands on the court and the line, as in Figure 6.5.

■ **Figure 6.5** Calling a ball out.

- Make any out call immediately.
- If you can't see whether a ball is definitely out, continue play-ing the point.
- A call can't be changed, even if a ball mark found after the point indicates a previous *shot* was out. The point stands as played.
- If you fail to see whether a ball that goes past you stays in or goes out, you must award the point to your opponent.
- A player loses the point for catching the ball on the fly, no mat-ter where the player thinks it might land and even if the player is standing outside of the court.

Doubles Play

Young tennis players enjoy playing one-on-one matches, but don't be surprised if many of your players prefer the game of doubles. In doubles, a player and a partner play against a pair of players on the other side of the net. To accommodate the extra players, the tennis court (see p. 70) is expanded to its full dimensions, from doubles sideline to doubles sideline. You must ensure that your players are aware of the following rules before they compete in doubles play.

- Either player on the team serving first may begin the match. Either person on the opposing team may receive the first ball in the right (or deuce) court.
- The receiving team may choose which player will play which court. They must then keep the same order of serving and the same sides for receiving for the whole set.
- If the server's partner is hit with the serve, a fault is called. If the receiver's partner is hit with the serve, the server wins the point.
- In returning shots (except the serve), either member of a doubles team may hit the ball. In other words, one partner may hit consecutive returns.

Court Conduct

It is imperative that you Comprehend the rules. However, the Communication and Character coaching tools are of equal importance in teaching players proper court behavior. You must both convey the importance of good conduct *and* exhibit it in your own actions if you expect your players to behave appropriately. Here is a checklist that you should encourage your players to follow:

- When standing near a tennis court in use, talk quietly so as not to disturb those who are playing (see Figure 6.6). Never walk behind a court in use until those playing have finished their point. This can be distracting to them.
- When you're ready to play, put racket covers, ball cans, jackets, and the like, out of everyone's way.

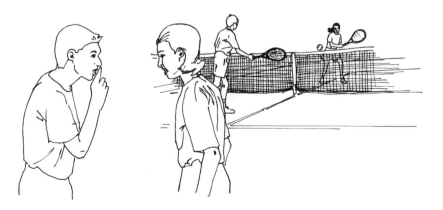

■ **Figure 6.6** Keeping quiet while others play.

- Introduce yourself to your opponent before warming up.
- Limit warm-up before a match to approximately 5 minutes. Hit balls back and forth with your opponent and take a few practice serves.
- In doubles, help your partner with line calls when possible. If your partner calls a ball out and you think it actually hit the line, you must call the ball good.
- Keep the game moving. Attempts to stall or to extend rest periods are illegal. Readily accept all calls made by your opponent.
- Intentional distractions that interfere with your opponent's concentration or effort to play the ball are against the rules.
- If a serve is out, don't return it. Just tap it gently into the net or let it go behind you.
- If the ball goes into the next court, wait until the players on that court finish their point before asking for the ball. If a ball from an adjacent court comes onto yours, return it as soon as play has stopped on both courts.
- If there is any disagreement on the score, go back to the last score you and your opponent agree on, or spin a racket, with the winner setting the score.
- After the last point, come to the net quickly and shake hands with your opponent (see Figure 6.7). Let your opponents

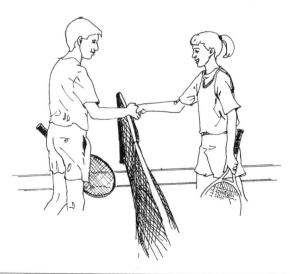

■ **Figure 6.7** Postmatch handshake.

know you appreciated the match, no matter what the outcome.

If players and their opponents cooperate in following the rules of tennis and treat each other with respect, they'll all get the most enjoyment from the game, whether they win or lose.

Summary Test

Now that you've read the basic tennis information in this unit, you should be able to answer a number of questions about the game. To test yourself, take the following quiz:

Tennis Court Matching Exercise
(refer to Figure 6.8)

1. _____ Center service line

2. _____ Baseline

3. _____ Right service court

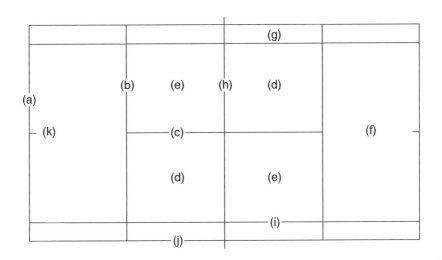

■ **Figure 6.8** Tennis court matching exercise.

Scoring: True or False

4. _____ When the server wins the first point of the game, the score is love-15.

5. _____ The score is 40-40. The next point determines the game winner.

6. _____ The score is 4-2, a total of six games. The set is finished.

Rules and Etiquette: Multiple Choice

7. _____ How many chances does a player have to hit a good serve before losing the point?

   a. one
   b. two
   c. three

8. _____ On return of serve, the receiver must hit the ball

   a. after it bounces once
   b. before it bounces
   c. either before or after it bounces once

9. _____ During a point, a ball that lands on the baseline is considered

   a. a let
   b. a fault
   c. a good ball

Answers: 1. c, 2. a, 3. d, 4. f, 5. f, 6. f, 7. b, 8. a, 9. c

Unit 7

What Tennis Skills and Drills Should I Teach?

Tennis is a sport that requires adept individual skills. A player with little understanding of or training in these techniques has little chance of success. Therefore, it is important that you instruct your players well in these tennis skills and organize drills effectively so they can develop them. This unit tells you how.

Racket Control

The most basic skill in tennis is the *stroke*, or swing. The most important element of any tennis stroke is the contact point, the point at which the ball meets the racket face. Regardless of a player's stroke pattern or body position, the ball will go wherever the racket face is pointing at contact. The grip a player uses determines the racket face angle at the contact point, so your players must know and use the proper grip for each stroke.

Grips

To know which grip to use for a stroke, players need to consider such factors as ball speed, height of bounce, spin, and where on the court they are making the shot. Players should experiment to find which of the basic grips—eastern, western, and continental—they are comfortable with and suits them best for each particular shot. After the players have established the basic forehand and backhand grips for their strokes, they can learn to vary these grips to handle different situations.

Ball Control

Once players are able to grip the racket properly and begin stroking the ball, you need to teach them proper shot placement. Here are five key concepts that will help your players learn and improve their control of the tennis ball.

Height—Because tennis is a net game, the first challenge in any stroke is getting the ball over the net. The height of the tennis ball is controlled by "opening" or "closing" the racket face. An open racket face points toward the sky, as shown in Figure 7.1a. A closed racket face points toward the ground, shown in Figure 7.1b. By contacting the ball with a slightly open racket face, the player will get the ball high enough to clear the net. If a player is continually hitting the ball into the net, instruct the player to open the racket face slightly at the contact point.

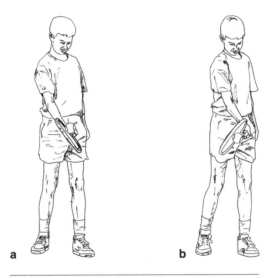

a   b

■ **Figure 7.1**   (a) Open racket face;
(b) closed racket face.

Direction—Help players learn how to place the ball in different parts of the court to move the opponent around. Again, the angle of the racket face at contact controls the direction of the ball. Teach players how to contact the ball with the racket face pointed to the right (the ball will go right) and to the left (the ball will go left). Then they'll be able to keep their opponents on the move.

Depth—To keep an opponent from attacking (moving toward the net), a player's shots must land deep in the court. The easiest and most consistent way to get sufficient depth is to hit the ball higher over the net. Work with players so they can achieve sufficient depth without hitting every shot beyond the baseline.

Power—Shot placement is more effective if the ball gets to the spot quickly, making it difficult for the opponent to return. The speed at which a ball travels is determined by the size and speed of the swing used to stroke the ball; a very short, slow swing produces a weak return, and a very large, fast swing generates a great deal of pace. However, warn players that as they increase the power of their strokes, they decrease their ability to control shots.

Spin—Using spin allows players to gain more control of their powerful shots. By imparting various types of spin, players no longer must rely solely on gravity to keep shots in the court. Thus, it's essential to teach players who wish to increase the accuracy of their more powerful shots how to use spin.

Making Contact

The key to all tennis strokes is when and where the racket makes contact with the ball. Players should prepare their swing early enough so they are able to make the racket contact the ball out in front of them. This means players should generally avoid taking an excessive backswing, which often results in the racket contacting the ball late, making it difficult to achieve control and pace. For each stroke, players should try to identify the ideal contact point. Basic groundstroke drills provide an excellent opportunity for players to develop consistent strokes.

How Do I Use Tennis Drills Effectively?

The key to using tennis drills effectively is to maintain control of each activity. Here are several tips for keeping drills under control:

- Make the purpose of each drill or activity clear.
- Give specific directions to players regarding such things as where to line up, what task is to be performed, and which court area to hit into.

- Randomly choose groups in a variety of ways—by best and worst at a particular skill, by overall ability, or by month of birth—to name a few. Change groups frequently to maintain enthusiasm.
- Ensure feeding of tennis balls is "friendly," with minimal tossing and retrieving.
- Set up targets for players to hit to (racket covers, towels, Frisbees).
- Use dead ball drills (after the player hits one ball fed by the coach, a second ball is fed) when introducing a skill.
- Advance to live ball drills (the ball is fed and kept in play) as players practice and improve.
- Make sure to offer positive reinforcement to players who are drilling whenever an opportunity arises.

Learning by Areas of the Court

The USTA National Coaches believe the drills and activities you select should encourage players to master their performances in each area of the court. For example, the net play lessons teach more than how to *volley*—they tell you how to instruct players to play the net. So even if you're a first-time coach, you can help your players learn to perform consistent and winning volleys and *overheads*. Here's the sequence to follow to develop your players' tennis skills for league play:

Baseline
1. Serve
2. Forehand groundstroke
3. Backhand groundstroke
4. Lob

Midcourt
5. Forehand
6. Backhand
7. Transition Game

Net
8. Volley
9. Overhead smash
10. Coverage

Doubles play
11. Serve & volley

Specialty shots
12. Spins

What Tennis Drills Should I Use?

The drills and activities in this section are designed for the average *USA Team Tennis* player who has played enough tennis to maintain brief rallies from baseline to baseline. For additional drills and activities for varying ability levels, contact the USTA.

PRACTICE #1

Baseline: The Serve

Performance Objective
Players will be able to hit full-swing baseline serves using the proper grip.

Introduce the Serve

Bring players into a semicircle around you.

1. Introduce yourself.
2. Summarize the objectives for the season: to have fun, increase consistency of all shots, begin to feel comfortable playing in all areas of the court, and develop new specialty shots like the spin serve.
3. Review key rules:
   - No hitting balls or swinging rackets until you give the word.
   - No talking when the team is called together.
   - When you address the team, everyone is to hold the racket against the chest with crossed arms (demonstrate).
4. Say, "For our first practice we are going to learn how to hit full-swing serves. The serve is the most important stroke in the game of tennis because it is used to start every point."

Demonstrate the Serve

From the service line, demonstrate three or four full-swing serves (see Figures 7.2, a-f) from various angles before your players. Show them how the serve resembles an overhand throw.

■ **Figure 7.2** The serve.

Explain the Serve

Point out the elements of the continental grip (see Figure 7.3), stance, backswing and toss, contact point, and follow-through. Urge players to develop a pre-serve ritual to help them relax and focus.

■ **Figure 7.3** The continental grip.

Attend to Players' Practicing

Warm-Up Activity: Groundstroke & Dig (4 minutes). Have players form a single-file line behind the baseline. One at a time, feed each player a forehand groundstroke and a drop shot to the backhand. Have players jog to pick up balls they've just hit and return to the end of the line (see Figure 7.4).

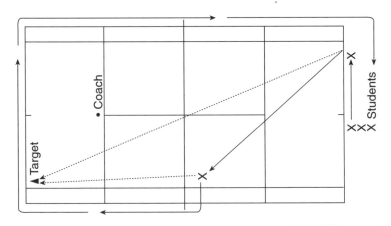

■ **Figure 7.4** Groundstroke and dig activity.

Stretching (6 minutes). Bring players into a circle around you to perform the stretches in unit 5 (pages 57-62). While all are stretching, ask players to introduce themselves in turn and summarize their tennis backgrounds.

Serve Drills

Serve Assessment (5 minutes). With players spread out along the baseline, observe their technique during warm-up serves. Take players having difficulty performing a proper full-swing serve through the Serve Progression. Those already comfortable with a full-swing serve should move to a separate court and complete the Parallel Activity.

> ➡ *Safety Tip.* Whenever players are lined up to hit full-swing serves, they must follow your commands on when to serve and when to pick up. This will prevent a player who is retrieving a ball from being hit by a server. Keep all other players well behind the servers until you tell servers to pick up their balls.

Serve Progression (12 minutes). Position players in up to four lines, perpendicular to the net. Have players observe your demonstration. Then have them model the following progression:

1. **Stance**—Stand sideways to net.

2. **Grip**—Hold racket up on edge toward net with nondominant hand and grip like a hammer with the racket hand.

3. **Backswing**—Drop both arms together and raise the racket arm to shoulder height with the knuckles pointed up and the racket pointed toward the back fence.

4. **Backswing, Bend, and Extend**—Take a backswing, bend the racket arm at the elbow, then extend upward with the racket hand facing the net (repeat).

5. **Backswing, Bend, Extend, and Shift**—Repeat the extension and add weight transfer from the back to the front foot by opening the hips toward the net and leaving only the toe of the back foot touching the ground.

6. **Backswing, Toss, and Tap**—Standing near the fence, take a backswing, toss a ball, and bend and extend the racket, tapping the ball against the fence. Check for proper grip and full extension (repeat).

7. Backswing, Toss, Tap, and Follow-Through—Have players form four lines behind the service line. The first player in each line stands four feet from the net and "tap-serves" four balls over the net, following through slowly across the body to the opposite hip. The player retrieves the four balls and returns to the end of the line.

8. Full Swing—Players slowly perform toss and full backswing, tap, and follow-through.

Parallel Activity: Target Serve. Position players in two single-file lines per court, behind the baseline. Each player serves four balls to a target placed in each service box, then goes to the end of the other line. When all balls have been hit, players pick them up and begin serving again. (If players request or need additional incentives, they can keep score, with one point for every successful serve and three points for hitting the target.)

Error Detection and Correction for the Serve

Error

1. Using an improper grip
2. Leading with the elbow
3. Having a hitch in the swing

Correction

1. Start with the continental and squeeze the grip when the racket passes behind the head.
2a. Use the proper grip.
 b. Reach up to contact, then serve and freeze at contact.
3a. Guide the player's arm through in slow motion.
 b. Perform two complete motions, one after the other, the first with no toss and the second with a toss and hit.

Serve Practice—Height Control (5 minutes). Have each player place four balls on the court: 4 feet from the net, on the service line, at 3/4 court, and on the baseline. On command, players serve the balls over the net, progressing from the net to the baseline. Once all balls have been hit, players retrieve and repeat. Stress using the proper serve grip.

➡ *Coaching Tip.* Successful servers get a high percentage of serves in the court. Remind your players that a few dazzling aces among several double faults are not nearly as effective as hitting serves that always go in and therefore must always be returned.

Serve & Return—Directional Control (6 minutes). Form two lines of servers on one side of each court and two lines of receivers on the opposite side. Each server hits two balls to the correct service box and goes to the end of the receiving line. Have teams switch roles so players can work on the opposite stroke.

Team Singles (10 minutes). Have equal groups line up single file behind the baseline and on opposite sides of the net. One at a time, each player plays one point of a singles game, then returns to the end of the line. Play as many games as time permits. If ample courts are available, have players play regular singles.

Serve & Return Game (10 minutes). Form two teams. Make half the players on each team servers and the other half receivers; line up the servers and receivers diagonally on opposite sides of the court. Each server hits a serve to a receiving teammate, who attempts to return it cross-court. If the server can touch the return without taking more than one step, his or her team earns one point. Have players switch roles so they can work on both serves and returns.

Tennis Bowling (10 minutes). Form two teams and set up tennis cans like bowling pins on the service court. Players take turns hitting one or two balls in the target area, trying to knock down cans with their serves. One person on each team acts as the "pin-setter" and rotates into the serving line after everyone serves.

Team Serving (10 minutes). Form two teams. The first player serves one ball. If it is good, the server goes to the end of the line, and the next person becomes the server. If the serve is a fault, the server retrieves a ball from a basket and tries again. The server gets three tries before a new person becomes the server. The first team with 10 successful serves wins.

Ball Reaction Drill (5 minutes). Position players in up to four lines, parallel to and facing the net. Facing players from the opposite side of the net, hold up one tennis ball. Tell players to shuffle from side to side, forward and back as you move the ball in those directions. Players shuffle for 20 seconds, rest for 20 seconds. Take players through the drill four times.

> ➡ *Sportsmanship Tip.* Models of Etiquette (5 minutes). Have two players play a mock singles game in front of the team to review scoring for both games and sets. Emphasize proper court etiquette.

Practice Evaluation and Cool-Down (5 minutes). With players in a semicircle facing you, have them perform some light stretches to cool down. Briefly review and evaluate the day's activities. Ask players to practice their serves 15 minutes each to the *deuce court* and *ad court*, with or without a partner, before the next practice session.

PRACTICE #2
Baseline: The Forehand Groundstroke

Performance Objectives
Players will develop correct technique for the forehand *groundstroke* using the proper grip and will continue to improve the serve.

Review the Serve
Briefly review the serving elements of continental grip, stance, backswing and toss, contact point, and follow-through. Ask who practiced their serves since the last session.

Introduce the Forehand Groundstroke

Say, "Today we will warm up, stretch, and then work on the forehand groundstroke." Tell your players the forehand groundstroke is used to strike a ball on the racket side of the body after it has bounced.

Demonstrate the Forehand Groundstroke

From the service line and with players standing in the *alley*, demonstrate a forehand drive (see Figure 7.5, a-e) by using a drop hit (dropping the ball to your racket side and stroking it over the net). Next, demonstrate the forehand return of serve with only a shoulder turn, contact, and follow-through.

■ **Figure 7.5** Forehand groundstroke.

Explain the Forehand Groundstroke

Point out the elements of the forehand "shake hands" grip (see Figure 7.6), ready position, shoulder turn, racket back and down, step adjustment, contact point, and follow-through.

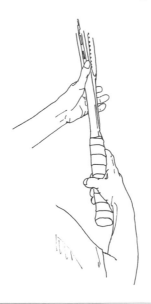

■ **Figure 7.6** Forehand grip.

Attend to Players' Practicing

Warm-Up Activity: Groundstroke & Dig (4 minutes).   See page 88.

Stretching (6 minutes).   See pages 57-62.

Forehand Progression (12 minutes).   Position players in up to four lines, perpendicular to the net. Demonstrate the forehand groundstroke. Then teach them the following progression:

1.   Ready Position—Stand midway between a forehand and a backhand, with feet pointing to the net and comfortably apart. Hold the racket comfortably in front at chest level, with the dominant hand on the grip and the nondominant hand either at the throat of the racket or also on the grip.

2.   Backswing—Release the nondominant hand, rotate shoulders to the forehand side while pivoting feet so body weight is centered over the back foot during the backswing. Keep the face of the racket perpendicular to the court.

3. **Contact Point**—Transfer body weight onto the front foot as the racket moves forward, with the racket arm fully extended. Stop swing with body weight on the front foot and the racket face pointed directly forward of the center of the court, just ahead of the front foot.

4. **Follow-Through**—Push the racket through the contact area and extend upward toward the target.

Forehand Drills

Forehand Practice (8 minutes). Two groundstrokers stand on the service line of the deuce and ad courts. Two feeders face them from the same position on the opposite side of the net. Two retrievers line up behind the feeders at the baseline. The feeder tosses the ball to the forehand side of the groundstroker, who hits a forehand down the line while concentrating on finishing with a long, high follow-through. Each groundstroker hits five balls and then moves to a retrieving position. The retriever moves to the feeding position and the feeder becomes a groundstroker. Have groundstrokers progress from service line to 3/4 court to baseline after each complete rotation.

Forehand Rallies (12 minutes). Players work six to a court. With partners across the net from each other in the doubles alleys and in the center of the court, have players complete the following forehand consistency progression:

1. In midcourt rallies, players work to hit 10 forehand groundstrokes in a row without an error.

2. Once a pair hits the ball 10 times in a row, they can back up to 3/4 court.

3. If they hit 10 forehands in a row from 3/4 court, both players move to the baseline and engage in full-court rallies. All shots must land beyond the service line. Challenge pairs to hit a record number of deep shots.

   ➡ *Safety Tip.* When positioned for drills, players must remain in their designated areas even if their balls leave their areas.

Bull in the Pen Game (5 minutes). Have players line up in a doubles alley on the service line. Toss a ball to a player who has moved to the center T for a forehand groundstroke. If the ball is hit successfully over the net, the player goes to the end of the line. Otherwise, the player goes to the opposite doubles alley (bull pen). Each player who hits a good shot goes to the end of the line, accompanied by the first person in the bull pen line. The game continues until everyone is in the bull pen or until everyone is in the original line.

Water Drill (5 minutes).   Have players line up single file behind the baseline. One at a time, each player stands at the baseline holding a cup of water. Feed them one ball for a forehand groundstroke and then toss them a second ball. Players must try to hit successful forehands without spilling any water.

Forehand Return of Serve (5 minutes).   Two hitters stand in returning position in the deuce and ad courts. Two servers stand on the opposite service line, with two retrievers behind them on the baseline, as shown in Figure 7.7. The server feeds the ball into the proper service box for the hitter to return cross-court. Retrievers pick up balls. Hitters return five forehands, then move to retrieving positions. Retrievers serve the balls they have picked up, and the servers become returners.

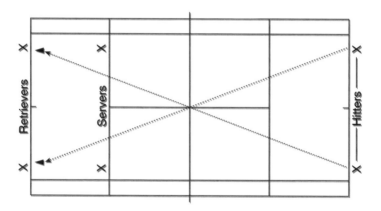

■ **Figure 7.7**   Forehand Return of Serve drill.

Rotating Team Rallies (5 minutes).   With teams lined up single file behind each baseline, put the ball into play with a drop hit from outside the doubles alley, near the service line. The first player in line hits a cross-court forehand and quickly returns to the end of the line so the next teammate may continue the rally. Teams score points for every ball hit successfully cross-court.

Serve & Forehand Rallies (5 minutes).   From the same formation used in the Forehand Return of Serve drill but with servers behind the baseline, players serve, return, and rally forehands cross-court for a record number of hits.

Conditioning—Toss & Catch (5 minutes). Divide team into pairs of tossers and catchers standing 6 feet apart and facing each other. Position pairs throughout the entire court area so they have plenty of space to move about. Holding two balls, the tosser tosses one ball between 1 and 6 feet in any direction. The catcher must quickly move to catch the ball after its first bounce and toss it back to the tosser. As soon as the catcher catches one ball, the tosser quickly tosses the second ball in another direction. Catchers catch for 20 seconds, then become tossers for 20 seconds. Take players through this rotation four times.

Practice Evaluation and Cool-Down (5 minutes). Review and evaluate the practice while players perform light stretches. Ask each player to set a record for continuous forehand rallies with a partner before the next practice. All balls must land in the singles court and must be returned on one bounce.

Error Detection and Correction for the Forehand

Error

1. Mistiming or overhitting shots
2. Lacking height or directional control

Correction

1. Shorten the backswing.
2a. Check for proper grip.
  b. Stop at contact to check the racket face.
  c. Follow-through high and toward the target.

➡ *Sportsmanship Tip.* Calling Lines (5 minutes). Have players stand on one baseline. On the opposite side of the court, place seven balls on and near the baseline. Ask players to make an "in" or "out" call on each ball using the proper hand signal. Indicate whether the ball was in or out after they make the call. Then have them walk around and see whether they were correct. They will better appreciate the difficulty in making calls from the opposite side of the net, even when a ball is stationary. Point out that because it is so hard to determine exactly where a ball lands from the other side of the net, they should not question opponents' calls.

PRACTICE #3
Baseline: The Backhand Groundstroke

Performance Objective
Players will develop correct technique for the backhand groundstroke using the proper grip.

Review the Forehand
Review the grip, ready position, shoulder turn, backswing, step adjustment, contact, and follow-through on the forehand groundstroke.

Introduce the Backhand

Say, "Today we will warm up, stretch, and then work on the backhand groundstroke. The backhand groundstroke is used to strike a ball on the nonracket side of the body after it has bounced."

Demonstrate the Backhand

With players standing in the doubles alley, show the one- and two-handed eastern backhand grips, as shown in Figures 7.8a and 7.8b. Check all grips; then, from the service line, using a drop hit, demonstrate the one-handed (see Figures 7.9, a-d) and two-handed (see Figure 7.10, a-d) backhand groundstrokes.

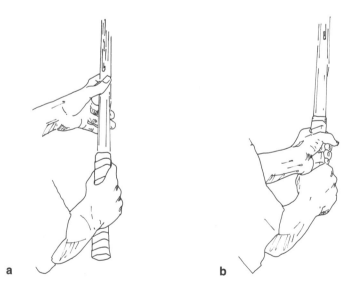

a   b

■ **Figure 7.8** Backhand grips: (a) one-handed; (b) two-handed.

a

b

c

d

■ **Figure 7.9**   One-handed backhand groundstroke.

■ **Figure 7.10** Two-handed backhand groundstroke.

Explain the Backhand

Explain the ready position, grip change as the racket is taken back with the thumb touching the opposite pocket, step adjustment, contact, and long follow-through. Players may use one- or two-handed backhands, but require all to make the proper grip change.

Attend to Players' Practicing

Warm-Up Activity: Forehand Rallies (4 minutes).   See page 95.

Stretching (6 minutes).   See pages 57-62.

Backhand Progression (12 minutes).   Position players in up to four lines, perpendicular to the net. Demonstrate the backhand. Then have players learn the following progression:

1.   Ready Position—Stand midway between a forehand and a backhand, with feet pointing to the net and comfortably apart. Hold the racket comfortably in front at chest level, with the dominant hand on the grip and the nondominant hand either at the throat of the racket or also on the grip (if using a two-handed backhand).

2.   Backswing—Rotate shoulders to the backhand side while pivoting feet so body weight is centered over the back foot during the backswing. Keep the face of the racket perpendicular to the court.

3.   Contact Point—With the front shoulder leading the elbow, transfer body weight onto the front foot and move the racket forward, with the racket arm fully extended. Stop swing with body weight on the front foot and the racket face pointed directly toward the center of the court, just ahead of the front foot.

4.   Follow-Through—Push the racket through the contact area and extend toward the target.

Backhand Drills

Backhand Practice (8 minutes).   Two groundstrokers stand on the service line of the deuce and ad courts. Two feeders face them from the same position on the opposite side of the net (same as Forehand Practice on page 95). Two retrievers line up behind the feeders at the baseline. The feeder tosses the ball to the backhand side of the groundstroker, who hits backhands down the line. Each groundstroker should hit five balls and then move to retrieving position. The retriever moves to the feeding position, and the feeder becomes a groundstroker. Have groundstrokers progress from service line to 3/4 court to baseline after each complete rotation. Stress a long, high follow-through on the stroke for proper ball height over the net.

> ➨ *Coaching Tip.* Most players find successful backhand shots harder to make than forehands. However, most experienced coaches find it easier to teach the backhand than the forehand, perhaps because there's much less variance in form among successful backhands. Using a two-handed backhand tends to bring players quicker success, so you should encourage it for those players experiencing major frustrations. If you teach proper technique (grip and stroke patterns), players can rapidly improve their backhand strokes.

Error Detection and Correction for the Backhand

Error

1. Leading with elbow
2. Lacking height or directional control

Correction

1. Place the thumb of the dominant hand on the opposite hip and "throw" the racket like a Frisbee.
2a. Check the grip.
 b. Stop at contact to check the racket face.
 c. Extend the follow-through high and toward the target.

Backhand Rallies (12 minutes).   Have players work six to a court. With partners across the net from each other in each doubles alley and in the center of the court (as in Forehand Rallies on page 95), have players complete the following backhand consistency progression (when forehands are hit they do not have to start over but may not count the stroke in their scores):

1. Have players begin with midcourt backhand rallies. Encourage players to hit 10 backhand groundstrokes in a row without an error.
2. Once a pair hits the ball 10 times in a row, they can back up to 3/4 court.

3. If they hit 10 backhands in a row from 3/4 court, both players can move to the baseline and engage in full-court rallies. All shots must land beyond the service line. Challenge pairs to hit a record number of deep shots.

Statue Game (5 minutes).   Have players line up in a doubles alley on the service line. Toss a ball to a player who has moved to the center T for a backhand groundstroke. If the ball is hit successfully over the net, the player goes to the end of the line. Otherwise, the player must freeze in the follow-through (like a statue). A player becomes "unfrozen" only when another player hits a successful backhand. The player who has been a statue the longest is the first to become unfrozen. Make sure you are aware of safe spacing as the players form statues.

T-E-N-N-I-S (10 minutes).   Form a group of four players. Pair off two players, and have them try to hit four shots each in a rally, using backhand groundstrokes only. If they reach that number, the group receives a letter *T*; if they do not reach that number, the next pair hits and tries for a *T*, and so on, until T-E-N-N-I-S is spelled.

Backhand Return of Serve (5 minutes).   Two hitters stand in returning position in the deuce and ad courts. Two servers stand on the opposite service line, with two retrievers behind them on the baseline (same as Forehand Return of Serve on page 96). The server feeds the ball into the proper service box for the hitter to return crosscourt. Retrievers pick up balls. Hitters return five backhands, then move to retrieving position. Retrievers serve the balls they have picked up, and the servers become returners.

Team Baseline Game (5 minutes).   Divide the group into two teams and have them stand well behind the baseline on opposite sides of the net. Two groundstrokers from each team stand on the baseline with teammates behind. Put the ball into play with a drop hit from outside the doubles alley near the service line. Players play out the point, two against two. When the point is completed, two new players from each team move up to the baseline to play the next point. Team scores are kept, with players rotating after every point.

➡ *Sportsmanship Tip.* Role-Playing to Teach (5 minutes).   An effective way to make a point about proper court conduct is to role-play the following two types of players. The first is a courteous, cooperative opponent who hits the ball under control in the warm-up and asks such questions as "Would you like to try some volleys?" The second is a player who is determined to smash every ball for a winner and complains every time the opponent doesn't get the ball back over the net. Ask your players which opponent they would prefer and why.

Conditioning—Roll & Catch (5 minutes).   Same as Toss & Catch on page 97, except the tosser rolls the ball on the ground. Take players through four rotations of rolling for 20 seconds and catching for 20 seconds.

Practice Evaluation and Cool-Down (5 minutes).   Review and evaluate the practice while players perform light stretches. Ask each player to set a record for continuous backhand rallies with a partner before the next practice. All balls must land in the singles court and must be returned on one bounce.

PRACTICE #4
Baseline: The Lob

Performance Objectives
Players will be able to execute the lob and will continue to improve groundstroke consistency.

Review the Backhand
Briefly review the grip, ready position, shoulder turn, backswing, step adjustment, contact, and follow-through on the backhand groundstroke.

Introduce the Lob

Say, "Today we're going to continue to work on groundstroke consistency and learn how to hit the lob." Explain that lobs are used by a player who is out of position or when an opponent is at the net.

Demonstrate the Lob

From the baseline, demonstrate both the forehand and backhand lobs from a drop hit.

Explain the Lob

Point out how the preparation for a lob is identical to a groundstroke but that the racket face is slightly open and the follow-through is higher for greater loft.

Attend to Players' Practicing

Warm-Up Activity: Backhand Rallies (4 minutes). See page 102.

Stretching (6 minutes). See pages 57-62.

Lob Drills

Lob Progression (12 minutes). Position players in up to four lines perpendicular to the net. Demonstrate the lob. Then teach them the following progression:

1. **Ready Position**—Stand midway between a forehand and a backhand, with feet pointing to the net and comfortably apart. Hold the racket comfortably in front at chest level, with the dominant hand on the grip and the nondominant hand either at the throat of the racket or also on the grip.

2. **Backswing**—Rotate shoulders to the forehand or backhand side while pivoting feet so body weight is centered over the back foot during the backswing. Keep the face of the racket perpendicular to the court.

3. **Contact Point**—Transfer body weight onto the front foot and move the racket forward, with the racket arm fully extended. Stop swing with body weight on the front foot and the racket face open to lift the ball up.

4. **Follow-Through**—Push the racket through the contact area and extend toward the target.

Clear the Coach (5 minutes). Players line up single file behind the ad court doubles alley. Feed one ball wide to the opposite corner; the first player runs the ball down and lobs over your head to a cross-court target. The player then quickly retrieves the ball just hit and returns to the end of the line (see Figure 7.11). Each player performs the drill five times. Move the line to the deuce court alley so players can work on the opposite stroke.

> ➡ *Coaching Tip.* Place targets (racket covers, Frisbees, or even towels) on the court for players to aim at during drills.

Change of Direction (5 minutes). Have players line up single file behind the ad court doubles alley. Feed three balls to the first player in line—down the middle of the court for a cross-court groundstroke, near the ad court sideline for a down-the-line groundstroke, and

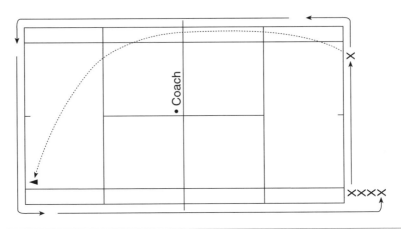

■ **Figure 7.11** Clear the Coach drill.

near the deuce court sideline for a lob. The player picks up the three balls just hit and returns to the end of the line. Each player performs the drill five times. Move the line to the deuce court alley so players can work on the opposite strokes.

> ➡ *Safety Tip.* When two players are on the court and others are waiting to step on, the observers must be careful to wait well in back of the baseline (so as not to interfere with play or get hit with a backswing), watching the action until it is their turn. Designate a safe waiting area for the on-deck team or player to keep players from crowding forward.

Alternate In (10 minutes). Place two players on each baseline and alternates standing between but well behind them (see Figure 7.12). Have players rally lobs cross-court. When a player makes an error, he or she is replaced by an alternate.

Alternate In With Serve (5 minutes). Same as the Alternate In drill, but players start the rally with a serve and return.

Team Singles (12 minutes). See page 91.

> ➡ *Sporstmanship Tip.* Spinning the Racket (2 minutes). Show players how to spin the racket to determine who will serve first in a match. Discuss the options of serving or receiving and choosing a side of the court or allowing your opponent to choose.

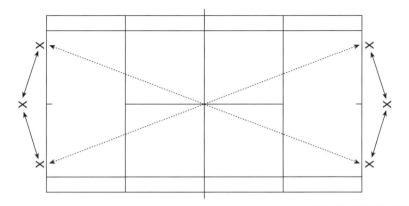

■ **Figure 7.12** Alternate In drill.

Conditioning—Toss, Roll, and Catch (5 minutes). Tosser randomly alternates tosses and rolls. Have players toss for 20 seconds, then catch for 20 seconds. Take players through this rotation four times.

Practice Evaluation and Cool-Down (5 minutes). Review and evaluate the practice while players perform light stretches. Ask each player to hit 20 cross-court drop hit lobs from both the forehand and backhand sides before the next practice.

Error Detection and Correction for the Lob
Error
No follow-through on the swing
Correction
Finish the stroke with the racket "high in the sky."

PRACTICE #5

Midcourt: The Forehand

Performance Objective
Players will be able to move from the baseline to the net area on the forehand side.

Review the Lob

Briefly review that a lob should be disguised by using the same preparation as a groundstroke, and it is used by a player who is out of position or when an opponent is at the net.

Introduce the Midcourt Forehand

Say, "Today we're going to learn how to play offensively on the forehand side by attacking short, weak returns and weak second serves."

Demonstrate the Midcourt Forehand

From the service line, demonstrate the three forehand shots that may be used in the midcourt area: a winner cross-court, an approach shot down the line, or a cross-court drop shot.

Explain the Midcourt Forehand

Point out a winner is a difficult shot to hit consistently, an approach shot is a high-percentage shot, and a drop shot should only be used as a surprise. Explain that all these shots require players to move through the shots using a shortened backswing. Players should aim for targets that risk only one line (few strategic shots demand hitting a ball close to two lines).

> ➡ *Coaching Tip.* Don't limit your instruction to groundstrokes from the baseline and volleys at the net; teach your players how to handle balls landing in the midcourt area. If your players feel comfortable with their midcourt skills, they will be better able to attack the net.

Attend to Players' Practicing

Warm-Up Activity: Forehand Rallies (4 minutes). See page 95.

Stretching (6 minutes). See pages 57-62.

Midcourt Forehand Drills

Forehand Winner (4 minutes). Have players form a single-file line behind the baseline. Feed a short, high forehand inside the service line. The first player in line hits to a cross-court target placed near the sideline and just beyond the service line. The first player then retrieves the ball and returns to the end of the line (see Figure 7.13).

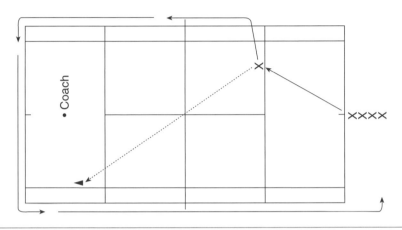

■ **Figure 7.13**   Forehand Winner drill.

Forehand Approach (8 minutes).   Form the same formation used in the Forehand Winner drill but, with a low bouncing feed, have players hit a controlled forehand down-the-line approach shot to a target placed near the baseline and several feet from the sideline. After a few rounds, feed a second ball to the players immediately after they hit the first approach shot. Have players hit a cross-court forehand (angle) volley to the corner of the service box on their second shots, as shown in Figure 7.14.

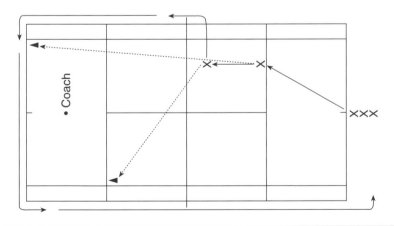

■ **Figure 7.14**   Forehand Approach drill.

Drop Shot (4 minutes). Using the same formation as the Forehand Winner and Forehand Approach drills and a medium height feed, have players hit a cross-court forehand drop shot that lands in the service box. Ask players to try to make the ball bounce three times before it leaves the service box.

> ➡ *Safety Tip.* When overhead smashes are hit as part of an activity, feed all balls from the bucket first, then have players pick up balls together. This will prevent players from being hit when retrieving balls.

Approach, Volley, and Overhead (5 minutes). Position players as in the Forehand Winner and Forehand Approach drills. Feed each player a forehand approach, forehand volley, and an overhead. The player then returns to the end of the line. Have everyone pick up balls when the bucket is empty.

Transition Workup (12 minutes). The object of this game is to work up to the feeder's side of the court and stay there as long as possible. The formation starts with two players on the baseline defending the singles court. Remaining players line up single file behind the opposite baseline. One of the baseline pair starts the point by feeding a short ball to the first player on the far side. The first player on the far side comes in and hits (based on the height of the bounce) an aggressive cross-court forehand, a down-the-line approach, or a drop shot, and plays out the point one against two. If the approaching player wins, she or he sprints around the net (to the right) and takes the spot of the nearest baseliner, who moves to her or his right. The baseliner who had been playing the right side runs to the back of the approaching line and starts over. If the approaching player loses the point, she or he goes to the end of the hitting line.

> ➡ *Sportsmanship Tip.* Fault and Let Serves (2 minutes). Briefly explain that a serve that touches the net and lands in the proper service box is called a let and must be replayed. If a serve goes into the net or does not land in the proper service box, a fault is called. Servers get two opportunities to serve into the correct service box on every point.

Conditioning—Toss, Roll, Catch, and Check (5 minutes). This drill is the same as the Toss, Roll, and Catch drill on page 107. However, the tosser occasionally yells "Check!" signaling the catcher to run up to and around the tosser and back to a position 6 feet away. Catchers catch for 20 seconds, then become tossers for 20 seconds. Take players through this rotation four times.

Practice Evaluation and Cool-Down (5 minutes). Review and evaluate the practice while players perform light stretches. Ask each player to play 10 consecutive points against a partner's midcourt forehand feed before the next practice.

Error Detection and Correction for the Midcourt Forehand

Error

Overhitting midcourt shots

Correction

Shorten the backswing by simply placing the racket face behind the ball, then following through.

PRACTICE #6
Midcourt: Backhand

Performance Objective
Players will be able to move from the baseline to the net area on the backhand side.

Review the Midcourt Forehand
Remind players of the forehand winner, approach shot, and drop shot options from the midcourt area.

Introduce the Midcourt Backhand

Say, "Now that you know how to play aggressively from the forehand side, we're going to practice the same shots from the backhand side."

Demonstrate the Midcourt Backhand

From the service line, demonstrate the winner, approach shot, and drop shot using both one- and two-handed backhands (see page 98).

Explain the Midcourt Backhand

As with the midcourt forehand, emphasize using a shortened backswing, moving through the ball, and aiming for targets.

Attend to Players' Practicing

Warm-Up Activity: Backhand Rallies (4 minutes). See page 102.

Stretching (6 minutes). See pages 57-62.

Midcourt Backhand Drills

Around the World (10 minutes). Form two single-file lines of players inside the opposing baselines near the center mark. The first player in one line starts the point with a groundstroke to the opposing player and then exits to the right and runs to the end of the line on the opposite side of the court. The player who returns the shot also exits to the right and runs to the end of the opposite line. Volleys are not allowed. Anyone who misses a shot is out and must leave the game. The last player left is the winner.

Backhand Winner (6 minutes). Players form a single-file line behind the baseline (see Forehand Winner, page 108). Feed one short, high backhand inside the service line, which the first player in line hits to a cross-court target placed near the sideline and just beyond the service line. The first player then retrieves the ball and returns to the end of the line.

> ➡ *Coaching Tip.* Players will often attempt to use the same long backswing in the midcourt area that they use from the baseline. Remind players that the closer they get to the net, the shorter the backswing must be.

Backhand Approach (8 minutes). Form the same formation used in the Backhand Winner drill, but with a low bouncing feed, have players hit a controlled backhand down-the-line approach shot to a target placed near the baseline and several feet from the sideline. After a few rounds, feed a second ball, which players hit as a cross-court backhand (angle) volley to the corner of the service box.

Drop Shot (4 minutes). Using the same formation as the Backhand Winner and Backhand Approach drills and a medium height feed, have players hit a cross-court backhand drop shot that lands in the service box. Ask players to try to make the ball bounce three times before it leaves the service box.

Approach, Volley, and Overhead (5 minutes). Form the same formation as the Drop Shot drill and feed each player a backhand approach, backhand volley, and an overhead; then have the player return to the end of the line. Have everyone pick up balls when the bucket is empty; continue the drill.

Transition Workup (12 minutes). See page 110. Players hit either forehand or backhand midcourt shots.

➡ *Sportsmanship Tip.* Calling Out the Score (2 minutes). Explain to players that as a courtesy and to avoid scoring problems during a match, the server calls out the score before every point.

Conditioning—React & Spring (5 minutes). Divide the team into pairs of tossers and catchers, standing 6 feet apart and positioned throughout the entire court area. Have catchers stand with their backs to the tossers. Instruct tossers to toss or roll the ball in any direction and call "Go!" Upon hearing the signal, catchers must turn, recover the ball, and turn away to listen for the next cue. Catchers catch for 20 seconds, and then become tossers for 20 seconds. Take players through this rotation four times.

Practice Evaluation and Cool-Down (5 minutes). Review and evaluate the practice while players perform light stretches. Ask each player to play 10 consecutive points against a partner's midcourt backhand feed before the next practice.

Error Detection and Correction for the Midcourt Backhand

Error

Opening shoulders and hips during the stroke

Correction

Stay sideways and use a carioca step (back foot crosses behind front foot) through the stroke.

PRACTICE #7
Midcourt: The Transition Game

Performance Objectives
Players will be able to hit a winner, an approach, and a drop shot from midcourt.

Review the Midcourt Backhand
Remind players of the backhand winner, approach shot, and drop shot options from the midcourt area.

Introduce the Transition Game

Say, "After a brief warm-up and stretch, we're going to continue to work on approaching the net when an opponent hits a short, weak return or second serve."

Demonstrate the Transition Game

From the service line, demonstrate the winner, approach shot, and drop shot from both the forehand and backhand (one- and two-handed) sides.

Explain the Transition Game

Remind players that a winner is a difficult shot to hit consistently, an approach shot is a high-percentage shot, and a drop shot should be used only as a surprise. Emphasize using a shortened backswing, moving through the ball, and aiming for targets.

Attend to Players' Practicing

Warm-Up Activity: Alternate In (4 minutes). See page 106.

Stretching (6 minutes). See pages 57-62.

Transition Drills

Winner (4 minutes). Have players form a single-file line behind the baseline (as in Forehand Winner on page 108). Feed a short, high forehand or backhand inside the service line, which the first player in line hits to a cross-court target placed near the sideline and just beyond the service line. The first player then retrieves the ball and returns to the end of the line.

Approach & Volley (5 minutes). Form the same formation used in the Winner drill, but with a low bouncing feed, have players hit a controlled forehand or backhand approach shot down the line to a target placed near the baseline and several feet from the sideline. Feed a second ball that the players angle-volley cross-court to the corner of the service box. After three rounds, have players first hit a cross-court groundstroke, then an approach, and finally a volley.

Groundstroke and Drop Shot (5 minutes). Using the same formation as the Winner and the Approach & Volley drills and a medium height feed, have players hit a cross-court groundstroke and a cross-court drop shot from either the forehand or backhand side.

Half-Court Approach (10 minutes). On one half of the court, have players form two single-file lines behind opposite baselines. The first players from each line begin a rally with a drop hit. Players rally, using only half the court, until one player makes an error or gets a short ball. The player receiving the short ball must hit an approach shot and play out the half-court point. Upon completion of the point, players return to the ends of their lines. When most of the players are successful, divide the team into four single-file lines and have two half-court points played at the same time.

> ➡ *Coaching Tip.* One of the big advances for a tennis player comes when he or she can transform a soft, short ball from a difficult get or an outright winner into an offensive opportunity. This has more to do with preparation, anticipation, and practice than raw speed.

Team Singles (10 minutes). Refer to page 91. Encourage players to attack at every opportunity.

Conditioning—Line Sprints (5 minutes). Using one doubles sideline as the starting line, have players sprint to and touch the first singles sideline, return to touch the starting line, sprint and touch the center service line, return, sprint and touch the far singles sideline, return, sprint and touch the far doubles sideline, and return to the starting line. Players sprint for 20 seconds, then rest for 20 seconds. Take players through this rotation four times.

Practice Evaluation and Cool-Down (5 minutes). Review and evaluate the practice while players perform light stretches. Ask players to play 10 consecutive points against a partner's midcourt feed before the next practice.

> ### Error Detection and Correction for the Midcourt Shots
>
> Error
>
> Stopping before hitting the shot
>
> Correction
>
> Push off the back foot and run through the stroke.

➡ *Sportsmanship Tip.* Continuous Play (2 minutes). Explain to your players that play in tennis must be continuous. This means players must warm up all their strokes, including serves, during the warm-up period, and they may take no longer than 30 seconds between points once play has begun.

PRACTICE #8
Net Play: The Volley

Performance Objectives
Players will be able to execute the forehand and backhand volleys.

Review the Transition Game
Remind players to approach the net when an opponent hits a short, weak return or second serve by using the winner, approach shot, or drop shot.

Introduce the Volley

Say, "During today's practice we're going to learn how to hit the volley." Point out that the volley is used when one is positioned at the net to hit the ball before it bounces. A player who can reach the net position during a point has a tremendous advantage. The net player has many more court angles to hit into, and the baseline opponent is forced to hit a difficult passing shot.

Demonstrate the Volley

Briefly demonstrate the ready position and crossover step as you block the ball on both the forehand and backhand volleys, as shown in Figures 7.15 and 7.16, respectively.

Practice #8

a   b

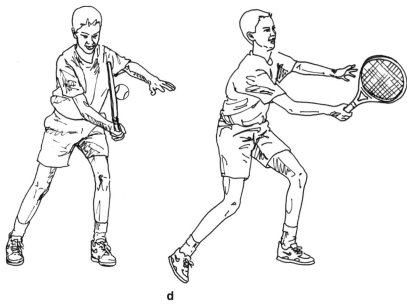

c   d

■ **Figure 7.15** Forehand volley.

■ **Figure 7.16** Backhand volley.

Explain the Volley

Explain that the eastern forehand and backhand grips may be used for volleys but little or no backswing is required for the stroke. Advanced players use a continental grip for both forehand and backhand volleys.

Attend to Players' Practicing

Warm-Up Activity: Groundstroke Rallies (4 minutes). Players may hit forehands or backhands (see pages 95 and 102).

Stretching (6 minutes). See pages 57-62.

Volley Drills

Volley Progression (12 minutes). Position players in up to four lines, perpendicular to the net. Demonstrate the volley. Then teach them the following progression:

1. Ready Position—Stand midway between a forehand and a backhand, with feet pointing to the net and comfortably apart. Hold the racket comfortably in front at chin level, with the dominant hand on the grip and the nondominant hand either at the throat of the racket or also on the grip.

2. Backswing—Rotate shoulders to the forehand or backhand side while pivoting feet so body weight is centered over the back foot, then make a short backswing. Keep the face of the racket head above the hand.

3. Contact Point—Transfer body weight onto the front foot and move the racket forward to block the ball at the front of the lead leg.

4. Follow-Through—Punch the racket through the contact area a short distance toward the target.

Volley Practice (8 minutes). Two volleyers stand in the service boxes of the deuce and ad courts. Two feeders face them from the same positions on the opposite side of the net. Two retrievers line up behind the feeders at the baseline. Feeders toss the ball alternately to the forehand and backhand sides of the volleyers, who hit volleys down the line. Each volleyer hits five balls and then moves to the retrieving position. The retriever moves to the feeding position, and the feeder becomes a volleyer.

Error Detection and Correction for the Volley

Error

1. Making contact behind the body on the forehand
2. Jabbing the volley on the backhand
3. Using the same racket face on both the forehand and backhand sides in a "windshield wiper" fashion

Correction

1. Cross the free arm over the hitting wrist.
2a. Keep the elbow fairly straight and make certain the thumb is wrapped around the grip.
b. Cradle the racket with the free hand.
3. Place a piece of tape on the edge of the racket and make certain the tape always faces up.

➡ *Coaching Tip.* As in the midcourt area, a common mistake made by players when volleying is to take too big a swing. Use key words or phrases like "block," "catch," and "squeeze and freeze" to remind players the volley requires little or no racket movement.

Two Volley (5 minutes). Have players form a single-file line in the ad court doubles alley behind the service line, as shown in Figure 7.17. Feed two volleys to the first player in line, the first near the

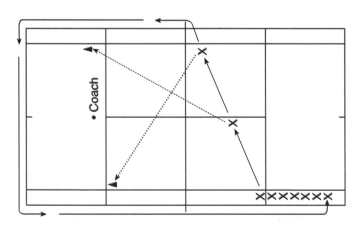

■ **Figure 7.17** Two Volley drill.

center service line and the second near the far sideline. The player hits the first ball to a target near the far sideline and angles the second ball to a target in the corner of the service box. The player moves diagonally toward the far net post to "cut off" both volleys, retrieves both balls, and returns to the end of the line. Each player performs the drill five times. Move the line to the deuce court doubles alley so players can work on the opposite stroke.

Groundstroke to Volley (10 minutes). Divide the team into single-file lines positioned behind the baseline and across the net behind the ad court service box, as shown in Figure 7.18. Feed a forehand and backhand groundstroke to the first baseline player, who hits each shot to the net player. The first player in the net-play line volleys each shot to a cross-court target. The groundstroker picks up two balls and moves to the end of the net-play line. After five rounds, move the net-play line to the deuce court so players can work on the opposite strokes.

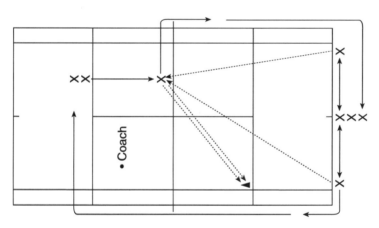

■ **Figure 7.18** Groundstroke to Volley drill.

➡ *Sportsmanship Tip.* Call Against Yourself (2 minutes). Explain that players are required to make calls against themselves on double bounces, upon touching the net, or on out balls that an opponent cannot or does not call against the player.

Kamikaze Volley (5 minutes). Form two single-file lines at each baseline. Have the first player in each line stand at 3/4 court and put the ball in play, hitting volleys only. Players must take one step toward the net after making a successful volley. Players remain on the court until they miss a volley.

Volley Workup (12 minutes). The object of this game is for players to work up to the feeder's side of the court, then stay there as long as possible. Position two players on one baseline to defend the singles court, with the remaining players lined up single file behind the opposite baseline. One of the baseline pairs starts the point with a drop hit down the center of the court. The first player on the far side, now standing on the service line, moves in to hit a volley and play out the point one against two. If the volleyer wins the point, he or she sprints around the net (to the right), and takes the spot of the nearest baseliner, who moves to her or his right. The baseliner who had been playing the right side runs to the back of the volleying line. If the volleyer loses the point, he or she goes to the end of the volleying line.

Conditioning—Line Sprints (5 minutes). See page 115.

Practice Evaluation and Cool-Down (5 minutes). Review and evaluate the practice while players perform light stretches. Ask each player to hit 10 volleys in a row against a wall from the forehand and backhand sides before the next practice.

PRACTICE #9

Net Play: The Overhead Smash

Performance Objective
Players will be able to hit an overhead smash.

Review the Volley
Briefly review using the crossover step and remind players not to use a backswing on the volley.

Introduce the Overhead Smash

Say, "Today we're going to continue to work on our volleys and learn to hit the overhead smash." Briefly explain that an overhead smash is used from the net to "put away" a lob.

Demonstrate the Overhead Smash

Have a player or assistant feed a few easy lobs for you to demonstrate the overhead smash from a position close to the net.

Explain the Overhead Smash

Describe the elements of the continental (serve) grip, ready position, pivot sideways to the net, racket back past the nose, track the lob with the free hand, adjust position beneath the ball, swing up toward the ball, and follow through across the body (see Figure 7.19). Point out the overhead is similar to the serve, except your opponent has placed the ball in the air, and you take the racket straight back behind the head instead of using a full swing.

a

b

c

d

■ **Figure 7.19**   Overhead smash.

Attend to Players' Practicing

Warm-Up Activity: Alternate In With Serve (4 minutes). See page 106.

Stretching (6 minutes). See pages 57-62.

Overhead Drills

Overhead Progression (12 minutes). Position players in up to four lines, perpendicular to the net. Demonstrate the overhead smash. Then have players learn the following progression:

1. Ready Position—Stand midway between a forehand and a backhand, with feet pointing to the net and comfortably apart. Hold the racket comfortably in front at chest level, with the dominant hand on the grip and the nondominant hand either at the throat of the racket or also on the grip.

2. Backswing—Raise racket into same position as for the serve, with shoulders and hips turned sideways to the net and body weight on the back foot. Use nonracket hand to point at the ball in the air.

3. Contact Point—Transfer body weight onto the front foot and bring the racket forward, with the racket arm fully extended, as in a serve.

4. Follow-Through—Finish swing with the racket following through the contact area and finishing on the opposite side of the body.

Overhead Progression (10 minutes). Place six to eight players on a court. On each side of the court (divided by the center service line extended), a retriever stands on one baseline, a feeder at 3/4 court, a hitter in the service box across the net, and a shadower on the opposite baseline, as shown in Figure 7.20. The feeder drop-hits three lobs to the hitter, the shadower mimics the hitter, and the retriever moves to the shadower position, the feeder to the retriever position, the hitter to the feeder position, and the shadower to the hitter position. Have players perform the following progression:

1. Pivot and catch the lob with the free, tracking arm.
2. Hit the overhead into the nearest doubles alley, touch the net, and prepare for the next overhead.
3. Hit one overhead in the air, one off the bounce, and another in the air.

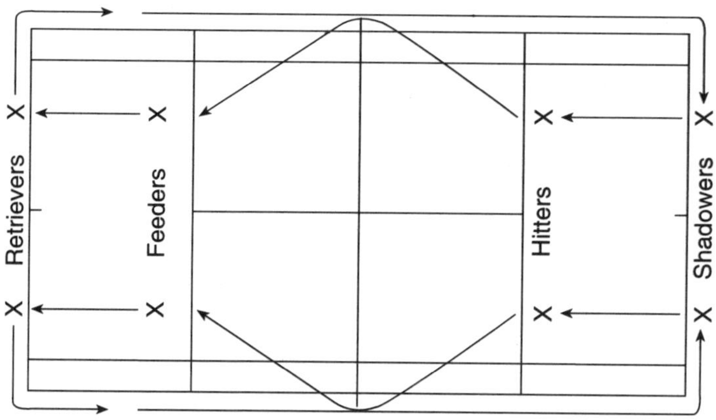

Figure 7.20 Overhead Progression drill.

Overhead Consistency (10 minutes). Position one player at the net and have the remaining players form a single-file line behind the baseline. Hit forehand and backhand lobs to the player at the net until a mistake is made; then it is the next player's turn at the net. The player who hits the most consecutive shots is the winner.

Volley, Touch, and Overhead (5 minutes). Position one player at the net and have the remaining players form a single-file line behind the baseline. Feed two balls to the net player, who hits a volley, touches the net with the racket, hits an overhead, and then returns to the end of the line. Have everyone pick up the balls when the bucket is empty. Each player performs the drill five times.

> ➡ *Coaching Tip.* Most players miss overheads by letting the ball drop too low or by swinging down on the ball. Instruct players to reach up as high as possible for contact and hit up and out when performing the smash.

Team Lob & Smash Game (10 minutes). Divide the group into teams of lobbers and smashers, who stand well behind the baseline on opposite sides of the net. Two smashers stand at the net, and two lobbers on the opposite baseline. A smasher begins the point with an easy drop hit to either lobber, who must attempt a lob. If a successful return is made using a lob, the lobbers score a point. The smashers score a point if the lobber fails to lob or by smashing away a short lob. When the point is completed, two new players from each team move into position to play the next point.

The game is completed when one team reaches 11 points; then have teams switch roles.

Team Singles (10 minutes). See page 91.

> ➡ *Sportsmanship Tip.* Long Serves (2 minutes). Tell players courtesy dictates they avoid returning long serves whenever possible by letting the ball pass by them or bumping the ball into the net. Then there will be no confusion over whether the serve was good, and players won't risk hitting an opponent who has looked away after seeing the serve was out.

Conditioning—Alley Hops (5 minutes). Have players hop over the doubles alley, with both feet together, from singles sideline to doubles sideline and back. Players hop for 20 seconds, then rest for 20 seconds. Take players through this rotation four times.

Practice Evaluation and Cool-Down (5 minutes). Review and evaluate the practice while players perform light stretches. Ask each player to hit a minimum of 20 overhead smashes before the next practice.

Error Detection and Correction for the Overhead Smash

Error
1. Backing up to reach a lob
2. Using a full swing

Correction
1. Turn sideways by stepping back with the racket-side foot and pivoting on the front foot, then shuffling back.
2. Take the racket back "past your nose, not your toes."

PRACTICE #10

Net Play: Coverage

Performance Objective
Players will develop greater consistency and coverage when playing the net.

Review of the Overhead Smash

Briefly review the similarities and differences between the overhead smash and the serve.

Introduce Net Coverage

Say, "After our warm-up and stretch, we're going to continue to work on covering the net."

Demonstrate Net Coverage

From a position halfway between the service line and the net, demonstrate how to use a crossover step toward the net to hit a forehand or backhand volley and then recover to the ready position.

Explain Net Coverage

Explain that by moving at a 45-degree angle toward the net, a player can cut off an opponent's passing shot.

Attend to Players' Practicing

Warm-Up Activity: Around-the-World Bump Volleys (4 minutes). Have players form a single-file line at the service line on each side of the net. Instruct the first player in line to "bump" a volley to the first player in the opposite line and quickly go to the end of his or her own line. Challenge players to hit a record number of volleys without letting the ball bounce.

Stretching (6 minutes). See pages 57-62.

Net Coverage Drills

Triangle (5 minutes). Have players form a single-file line behind the baseline. The first player in line moves up to the service line, as shown in Figure 7.21. Feed the player a volley near the right sideline, a volley down the center of the court, and an overhead. The player then picks up the three balls and returns to the end of the line. Each player should do the drill five times going to their right. Next, feed the first volley to the players' left so they can work on the opposite strokes.

Alternate In: Groundstroke to Volley (10 minutes). Two players stand at the net with alternates behind the service line and two

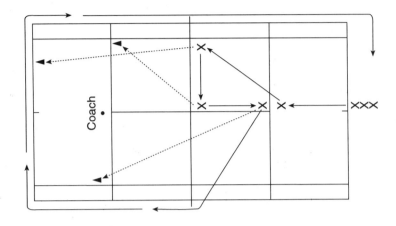

■ **Figure 7.21** Triangle drill.

players at 3/4 court across the net with alternates behind the baseline. Players rally cross-court, groundstroke to volley. When a player makes an error, he or she is replaced by an alternate. After several rotations, have the groundstrokers move to the baseline. After five minutes, reverse the players' roles so they can work on the opposite shot.

Net Play Workup (10 minutes). See Volley Workup on page 122. Encourage baseline players to mix in lobs and groundstrokes.

Alternate In: Continuous Volley (10 minutes). A player stands in each service box with alternates behind the service lines. Players hit volley to volley (not letting the ball bounce) cross-court. When a player makes an error, she or he is replaced by an alternate.

➡ *Sportsmanship Tip.* Postmatch Conduct (2 minutes). Review the proper conduct for both the winner and loser of a match, including shaking hands.

Conditioning—Alley Hops (5 minutes). See page 126.

Practice Evaluation and Cool-Down (5 minutes). Review and evaluate the practice while players perform light stretches. Ask each player to hit 20 consecutive groundstroke-to-volley rallies with a partner from the forehand and backhand sides before the next practice.

Error Detection and Correction for Net Coverage

Error
Moving parallel to the net to reach a volley

Correction
Crossover step at an angle toward the net to cut off the volley.

PRACTICE #11
Doubles Play: The Serve & Volley

Performance Objective
Players will begin to charge the net following their first serve in doubles.

Review Net Coverage
Remind players to move at an angle toward the net to cut off passing shots.

Introduce the Serve & Volley

Say, "After the warm-up, we are going to learn the serve and volley tactic for doubles." Point out that the most successful doubles teams are those who rush the net and volley away their opponents' returns.

Demonstrate the Serve & Volley

Demonstrate the serve and volley using a split-step at the service line and volleying cross-court.

Explain the Serve & Volley

Point out that when both players of a doubles team are at the net, they have many more court angles to hit into, which gives them a greater chance of winning the point. Doubles teams that can charge the net behind their serves gain an immediate advantage. Relate the split-step to a landing in hopscotch. It allows a player to remain balanced while adjusting to volley an oncoming return of serve.

Attend to Players' Practicing

Warm-Up Activity: Alternate In: Groundstroke-to-Volley (4 minutes). See page 127.

Stretching (6 minutes). See pages 57-62.

Serve & Volley (10 minutes). Stand in the deuce court receiving position with one player serving to you, one partnering the server at net, and one as your partner on the ad court service line, as shown in Figure 7.22. The remaining players wait behind the server. The server serves to you and rushes to the net, split-stepping at the service line. Let the serve go by and feed a drop hit cross-court return. The server volleys the return, and the point is played out. Upon completion of the point, the server moves to the net position, the net player runs around to become your partner, and your former partner goes to the end of the serving line.

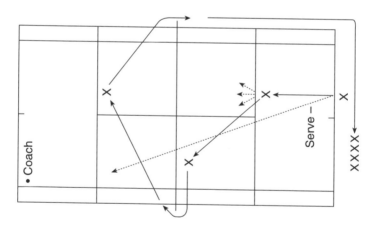

■ **Figure 7.22** Serve and Volley drill.

➡ *Safety Tip.* Teach doubles partners to shout "Mine!" on any balls hit down the middle. The first player to call plays the shot. This prevents both players from swinging at the same ball, possibly injuring each other.

Team Volley Game (10 minutes). Divide the group into two teams, which stand well behind the service line on opposite sides of the net. Two volleyers from each team stand in each service box with teammates behind. Put the ball into play with a drop hit from outside the doubles alley near the service line. Players play out the point volley to volley, two against two. When the point is completed, two new players from each team move up to the service boxes to play the next point. Keep team scores, with players rotating after every point.

Monarchs of the Court (15 minutes). This is a progressive workup game in which players play 12-point tie-breaker doubles "matches." The goal of the game is to work to the "top of the hill" and stay there by beating challengers. Place two doubles teams on each court and designate one court as the champion's court. All winners will move toward this court (see Figure 7.23). Losers on all but the champion's court remain and serve the next point. Losers on the champion's court go to the end of the line at the beginning of the rotation. Teams waiting to challenge should wait by the net post so they can simply step onto the open side of the court while the champion team gets balls ready to serve.

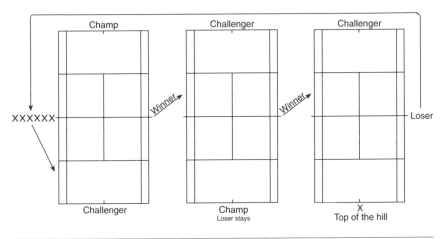

■ **Figure 7.23** Monarchs of the Court drill.

Error Detection and Correction for Doubles

Error

1. Mistiming the split-step
2. Returners trying to pass the net players

Correction

1. Hopscotch when opponent makes contact with the return.
2. Hit lobs over net rushers' heads and take over the net.

➡ *Sportsmanship Tip.* Encouraging Doubles Partners (2 minutes). Describe to players how doubles partners can either hinder each other with berating comments or help each other with positive ones (e.g., "Don't worry, we'll get the next one." Or "Hang in there. All we can do is try as hard as we can!").

Conditioning—Toss, Roll, and Catch (5 minutes). See page 107.

Practice Evaluation and Cool-Down (5 minutes). Review and evaluate the practice while players perform light stretches. Ask each player to play one set of doubles before the next practice.

PRACTICE #12
Specialty Shots: Spins

Performance Objectives
Players will begin to develop underspin and topspin groundstrokes and slice serves.

Review of the Serve & Volley
Remind players of the advantage achieved when they follow their serves to the net in doubles.

Introduce the Skill

Say, "Today we will learn three types of spin and how to apply them." Emphasize that one of the marks of a player moving to more advanced tennis is understanding the use of spin.

Demonstrate the Skill

Show players how to hit "ups" with *underspin* by brushing beneath the ball; occasionally let the ball bounce to show what effect the spin has. Next, demonstrate *topspin* by rolling a ball on the court, then hitting a drop hit topspin forehand. Finally, hit a *slice* serve to show players how the ball curves through the air.

Explain the Skill

Explain that a ball can be hit with underspin by using a U-shaped (high to low to high) swinging pattern and brushing beneath the ball. Topspin is created by brushing up behind the ball with a low to high swing.

To describe a slice serve, ask players to imagine there is a face painted on the ball (or actually draw one). Explain that a flat serve is one in which the racket hits the "face" on the nose. A slice serve is performed by brushing across the "ear" of the ball. Point out they must use the continental (serve) grip to accomplish the slice serve.

Attend to Players' Practicing

Warm-Up Activity: Groundstroke Rallies (4 minutes). See pages 95 and 102.

Stretching (6 minutes). See pages 57-62.

Ups With Underspin (2 minutes). Have players spread out over the entire court area and perform ups with underspin. Ask them to occasionally let the ball bounce to see the effect of the spin.

Alternate In With Underspin (5 minutes). Have players hit cross-court underspin groundstrokes from the service line.

Topspin Forehand Progression (10 minutes). Circulate and encourage players to think of brushing up behind the ball as they complete the following progression:

1. Players pin a ball to the top of the net with the racket and then shoot it over the net by pulling the racket straight up to the shoulder (a *net brush*).
2. After five net brushes, players perform five topspin forehands with a drop hit over the net to a partner.
3. Players perform the Forehand Practice drill (page 95) using topspin forehands.

Slice Serve Practice (5 minutes). Have each player place balls 4 feet from the net, on the service line, at 3/4 court, and on the baseline. Instruct players to serve each ball over the net with spin by brushing along the "ear" of the ball, progressing from near the net to the baseline. Once all balls have been hit, players retrieve them and repeat the progression.

➡ *Coaching Tip.* By this stage of the game, many players will have developed strokes with a variety of spins, even without knowing it. Try to build upon these tendencies. Other players will have developed enough pace on serves to be having difficulty controlling them. These players need to add spin to both first and second serves.

Doubles With Spin (10 minutes). Divide the group into doubles teams and play regular games, requiring players to hit all first serves with spin.

Around-the-World With Topspin (5 minutes). Divide the team into two equal lines, which stand well behind opposite baselines. The first player in each line stands on the baseline. Feed the ball to one of the baseline players with a drop hit from outside the doubles alley near the service line. The baseline player must attempt to hit a topspin forehand over the net and run to his or her right to the end of the opposite line. A player making an error receives one "strike." A player with three strikes is eliminated from the game. Play continues until only one player is left.

Conditioning—Line Sprints (5 minutes). See page 115.

Practice Evaluation and Cool-Down (5 minutes). Review and evaluate the practice while players perform light stretches. Ask each player to practice slice serving for 20 minutes, mixing in regular serves, before the next practice.

Error Detection and Correction for Spins

Error

1. Hitting spin serves into the net
2. Spin serves veering too far left or right
3. Rolling the racket over the ball on topspin forehands
4. Chopping down on the ball on underspin backhands

Correction

1. Aim much higher than on a flat serve.
2. Adjust targets to account for the spin.
3. Brush up behind the ball for topspin.
4a. Keep a firm elbow.
 b. Swing from the shoulder in a U-shaped fashion.

Unit 8

How Do I Get My Players to Play as a Team?

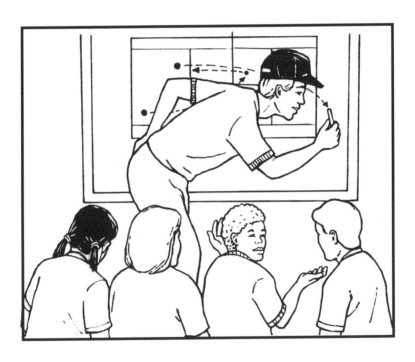

It is very important to emphasize development of individual skills when coaching young tennis players. You can enhance that development by having your youngsters practice and compete as a team.

Building a Tennis Team

The team setting provides an excellent opportunity for youngsters to develop as people and players in a less threatening group situation. USTA National Coaches recommend the following approaches for building a strong, positive team tennis environment.

1. Choose a team name and motto. Have your players select a name for the team and a motto (e.g., "Face the Pace!") that can be repeated during practices and matches. This will help players feel a special identity with the squad.

2. Provide a team uniform. It's important for players to have some visual identification that shows they belong. Having the same T-shirts or other uniform apparel will make everyone feel a part of the team.

3. Require player support. As a rule, every player should be required to watch teammates' matches in a supportive, positive manner, regardless of the position of the player or importance of the match to the team's overall score. This fosters team loyalty and spirit.

4. Establish a team ritual. Team practices and matches should begin and end with the team in a group and should follow a set ritual. You may wish to give a few encouraging words, have the team put their hands together, and repeat the team motto together.

5. Have fun off the court. Have your team participate in nontennis activities together. Attend a carnival, go to a museum or zoo, take a bike trip, or play another team sport together. This will allow players to get to know each other even better by interacting away from the tennis court.

Prematch Planning

In unit 4 we discussed the importance of planning your practices. Similar preparation is required for team matches. Your team and their opponent will get the most out of the *USA Team Tennis* match experience if the competition is well organized and well run.

1. Scheduling. Write down the schedule of play for the upcoming match. It's generally best to schedule doubles matches before singles matches so more kids get to participate on the courts at the start. When you're certain of the match schedule, confirm court availability with the staff of the facility where you will be playing.

2. Calling the opposing coach. Contact the opposing coach at least 2 days before your teams are to play to confirm the date and time of the match, directions to the tennis facility, number of courts to be used, and the schedule of play. In case of threatening weather, stay in touch with the opposing coach to decide on postponement or rescheduling.

3. Arranging for transportation. See that all your players get to the matches. Whenever possible, have your team travel to the match together and return together. Organize car pools for away matches, setting departure and arrival times so drivers and players know when and where to meet. Arrange for players to arrive at least 30 minutes before match time so they will have time for a proper warm-up. Players should also be taken home by the same driver.

4. Making lineup decisions. Depending on the format used in your area league, you will probably need to make some decisions as to who will play in what position. You'll need to decide who will play singles, who will play doubles and with whom, and in what order they will compete. Intrasquad scrimmages will help you determine players' relative order of ability, which in turn will help you set your lineup. Remember, one component of the *USA Team Tennis* philosophy is *Equal Play,* so make sure everyone plays either singles or doubles in each team match.

Match Day Duties

If yours is the home team, arrive at the match site at least 40 minutes before match time. Also:

1. Check facilities and equipment. Check the courts and nets for cleanliness and repair, get out the tennis balls for play, and make certain that water and a first-aid kit are available.

2. Communicate with participants. Greet the opposing team and coach as they arrive and allow them to warm up by sharing courts with your players. Before the start of the match, gather your team for a brief meeting to discuss the lineup, court assignments, and good sportsmanship. Next, gather both teams for the official lineup exchange.

3. Report the scores. Probably the single greatest headache for a league commissioner is collecting match scores in a timely fashion. To help your commissioner keep accurate and up-to-date records of match results, report all scores *immediately following* the completion of a team match.

Glossary of Tennis Terms

ace: A ball that is served so well that the opponent cannot return it.

ad (short for *advantage*): The point scored after deuce. If the serving side scores, it is *ad in*; if the receiving side scores, it is *ad out*.

all: An even score (30-all, 3-all, etc.).

alley: The area between the singles and doubles sidelines on each side of the court. (The singles court is made wider for doubles by the addition of the alley.)

approach: A shot hit just before a player comes to the net that puts the opponent on the defensive.

backcourt: The area between the service line and the baseline.

backhand: The stroke used to return balls hit to the left side of a right-handed player and to the right side of a left-handed player.

choke up: To grip the racket up toward the head.

cross-court shot: A ball hit diagonally across the court.

deep serve: A serve that bounces in the service court near the service line.

deep shot: A shot that bounces in play near the baseline.

deuce: A score of 40-40 (the score is tied and each side has won at least 3 points).

deuce court: The right court, so called because on a deuce score the ball is served there.

double fault: The failure of both service attempts; the server loses the point.

doubles: A match with four players, two on each team.

down-the-line shot: A ball that follows the path of a sideline and is close to it.

drop shot: A ball falling quickly into the forecourt after crossing the net.

fault: A service out.

15: The first point won by a player.

flat shot (flat serve): A shot that travels in a straight line with little arc and little spin.

foot fault: A fault called against the server for stepping on the baseline or into the court with either foot during the serve.

forecourt: The area between the service line and the net.

forehand: The stroke used to return balls hit to the right of a right-handed player and to the left of a left-handed player.

40: The score when a player has won 3 points.

game: The part of a set that is completed when one player or side wins 4 points, or 2 points in a row after deuce.

good ball: A ball in play that lands in the court (or on any part of a line forming the boundary of the court).

groundstroke: A stroke, forehand or backhand, made after the ball has bounced.

half-volley: A stroke made by hitting a ball immediately after it has touched on the ground.

let: A point played over because of interference. Also, a serve that hits the top of the net but is otherwise good, in which case the serve is taken again.

lob: A groundstroke that lifts the ball high in the air, usually over the head of the net player.

lob volley: A volleying stroke hit over the head of the opponent.

love: Zero (no score).

net game: Play in the forecourt close to the net.

no-ad: A system of scoring a game in which the first player to win 4 points wins the game. If the score reaches 3-all, the next point decides the game.

out: A ball landing outside the boundary lines of the court or, on the serve, outside the boundary lines of the receiver's service court.

overhead: A stroke made with the racket above the head.

poach: To hit a ball in doubles, usually at the net, that normally would have been played by one's partner.

point: The smallest unit of score, awarded to a player when the opponent does not make a good return.

rally: A series of good hits made successively by players. Also, the practice procedure in which players hit back and forth to each other.

receiver: The player who receives the service.

serve (short for *service*): The act of putting the ball into play for each point.

server: The player who serves.

service break: A game won by the opponent of the server.

set: A scoring unit awarded to a player or team who has won (a) six or more games and has a two-game lead, or (b) six games and the tie-break game when played at 6-all.

shot: The hitting of the ball across the net and into the court on the other side.

singles: A match between two players.

slice: To hit a ball with sidespin, like the spin of a top.

smash: A hard overhead shot.

spin: Rotation of the ball.

stroke: The act of striking the ball with the racket.

30: The score when a player has won 2 points.

tie-break game (tie-breaker): A system used to decide a set when the score is 6-all.

topspin: Forward rotation of the ball caused by brushing from low to high behind the ball.

underspin: The backward rotation of the ball caused by hitting high to low under the ball. Also, backspin or cut.

volley: A stroke made by hitting a ball before it has touched the ground.

ASEP Volunteer Level

The American Sport Education Program (ASEP) offers three Volunteer Level curriculums for adults who work with youth sport:

■ SportCoach   ■ SportParent   ■ SportDirector

SportCoach

ASEP's SportCoach Program consists of two courses:

The **Rookie Coaches Course** provides inexperienced coaches with essential information for teaching the skills and strategies of a sport, including sample practice plans. Companion coaching guides are available for baseball, basketball, football, gymnastics, hockey, ski racing, softball, soccer, swimming, tennis, volleyball, and wrestling.

The **Coaching Young Athletes Course** is for second-year coaches and others who want more instruction in the principles of coaching than is offered in the Rookie Course.

SportParent

ASEP's SportParent Course is a 1- to 2-hour program that provides youth sport administrators and coaches with a practical and effective way to educate parents about their children's participation in sports.

The SportParent Course Package includes the *SportParent Facilitator Manual,* the *SportParent Video,* the *SportParent Survival Guide,* and the *SportParent* book.

SportDirector

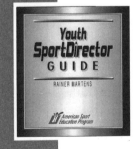

ASEP's SportDirector Program offers outstanding opportunities for youth sport directors to improve sport programs for the children in their community. The program includes a very practical *Youth SportDirector Guide* and a dynamic workshop.

American Sport Education Program

P.O. Box 5076
Champaign, IL 61825-5076
Fax: 217-351-1549

**For more information
on ASEP's Volunteer Level
programs, call Toll-Free
1-800-747-5698.**

More essential resources for tennis coaches

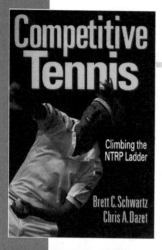

This book will speed anyone's climb up the National Tennis Rating Program (NTRP) ladder. Provides tools to rate students and includes advice to help them benefit from the most effective handicapping system in tennis—the NTRP. Also features drills and strategies for both singles and doubles.

1998 • Paper • 272 pp • Item PSCH0755
ISBN 0-88011-755-9 • $17.95 ($25.95 Canadian)

Hosted by Paul Roetert, the director of Sport Science for the USTA, this video presents a training program that puts players in top shape for maximum performance. The video shows proper technique for essential tennis conditioning exercises that lead to better performance on the tennis court.

1997 • 25 minutes • Item MUST0918
ISBN 0-88011-918-7
$24.95 ($37.50 Canadian)

30-day money-back guarantee.   Prices subject to change.

HUMAN KINETICS
The Premier Publisher for Sports & Fitness
http://www.humankinetics.com/